Electronic Payment Systems

Electronic Payment Systems

Winning new customers

James Essinger
James Essinger Associates, Canterbury, UK

CHAPMAN & HALL
University and Professional Division

London · Glasgow · New York · Tokyo · Melbourne · Madras

Published by Chapman & Hall, 2–6 Boundary Row, London SE1 8HN

Chapman & Hall, 2–6 Boundary Row, London SE1 8HN, UK

Blackie Academic & Professional, Wester Cleddens Road, Bishopbrigs, Glasgow G64 2NZ, UK

Chapman & Hall, 29 West 35th Street, New York NY10001, USA

Chapman & Hall Japan, Thomson Publishing Japan, Hirakawacho Nemoto Building, 6F, 1–7–11 Hirakawa-cho, Chiyoda-ku, Tokyo 102, Japan

Chapman & Hall Australia, Thomas Nelson Australia, 102 Dodds Street, South Melbourne, Victoria 3205, Australia

Chapman & Hall India, R. Seshadri, 32 Second Main Road, CIT East, Madras 600 035, India

First edition 1992

© 1992 James Essinger

Typeset in 11/13 Palatino by Intype, London
Printed in Great Britain by T. J. Press (Padstow) Ltd, Cornwall

ISBN 0 412 46290 7

A catalogue record for this book is available from the British Library

Library of Congress Cataloging-in-Publication data available

Contents

Acknowledgements

My principal acknowledgement is to Rob Farbother, founder and chief executive of Nexus Payment Systems International, who was most generous with his time, research material, and contacts. I also extend my gratitude and thanks to electronic payment systems marketing expert Julian Goldsmith, and consumer affairs guru Jeremy Mitchell.

Finally, I would like to thank Alan Nelson, my editor at Chapman & Hall, for his insight and imagination, and overall commitment to the project.

James Essinger
Canterbury

Preface

This book explains how electronic payment systems can help your retail bank or financial institution win new customers and, equally important, keep them.

In this book, an 'electronic payment system' is defined as a method by which customers of retail financial institutions can gain electronic access to their accounts, whether that access is made in order to gain information about the state of the account, or to undertake a transaction, such as a cash withdrawal, deposit, or payment delivery. In some cases (e.g. transactions across shared Automated Teller Machine (ATM) networks or across shared Electronic Funds Transfer at Point of Sale (EFTPoS) systems) interbank funds transfers will be involved, but this book focuses exclusively on electronic payment systems from the customer's point of view.

In the 20 years or so since electronic payment systems first began to be used, they have, in a very real sense, changed the face of the retail banking industry. Nonetheless, many bankers do not really understand that the prime motivation for deploying these systems should not be to make the banker's job easier, or to reduce the volume of the paperwork that flows through the branch, but to make the retail institution's products and services more attractive to customers, and to construct systems through which these more attractive products and services can be delivered.

This, I admit, is a somewhat revolutionary approach to electronic payment systems. You may have been used to regarding electronic payment systems as conferring a number of benefits, of which winning new business is only one.

In *Electronic Payment Systems*, I argue not only that the increased opportunity to win new business is by far the *most important* benefit of deploying these systems, but also that by making the winning of new customers your principal aim you are more likely to deploy effective and workable systems. You may, at the moment, disagree with all, or some, of this. I hope, by the end of the book, to win you over to my way of thinking.

The book also features extensive guidelines to implement the different systems most effectively and to extract the maximum level of competitive advantage from the implementation.

I believe very strongly that this knowledge is essential for everyone involved in the retail financial sector, not just people whose jobs take them into the specific arena of electronic payment systems. Five years of writing about and researching into electronic payment systems have taught me that the only feasible way for financial institutions to manage the process of change that is required by the new opportunities presented by electronic payments systems is to move towards new operational structures which incorporate these systems. These new operational systems naturally affect all staff of the retail financial institution which is deploying them. Furthermore, an integration of operational systems and electronic payments systems is essential. Merely hoping to 'tack on' the payment systems infrastructure to an institution's existing structure is unlikely to work, as it will not give the institution the opportunity to restructure its overall operations, promotional initiatives and general marketing in order to gain the greatest competitive advantage from deploying an electronic payments system.

And gaining a competitive advantage is precisely what implementing electronic payments systems is all about. One of the most significant changes in the retail financial sector since the 1960s has been a hugely increased willingness on the part of the customer to move from one financial institution to another, depending on which institution provides the best deal. The customer is increasingly likely to assess the deal in detail, both in terms of the rate of interest offered for savings, and the facilities – in particular access to electronic payments systems – which are offered with the account.

This willingness on the part of customers to migrate from one institution to another in search of a better deal is so familiar to us now that it is easy to forget that ever since the formal creation, in the late Middle Ages, of organizations that were the ancestors of modern banks, financial institutions have been remote, staunchly conservative establishments, where to be accepted as an account holder was a privilege and where few, if any, account holders would think of changing from one institution to another. In the UK, for example, operating a bank account remained a prerogative of the more wealthy members of society until the 1950s. It is only since the 1960s – and particularly since the widespread introduction of technology within the industrialized nations' banking sectors – that 'having a bank account' has become seen not only as a right rather than a privilege, but also as an opportunity for a customer to indicate customer preference.

The relationship between electronic payments systems and the customer is central to this book. I firmly believe that the successful implementation of electronic payments systems is very much a matter of meeting the needs of customers and accepting that it is customers – rather than the institution deploying the system – who hold the key to the future of the retail financial sector.

Above all, I believe that it is a prime requirement for anybody involved in the retail financial sector to remain constantly alive to the danger of being seduced by the idea that it is the *technology*, and not the customer-oriented market-place, which determines the success of an implementation of a particular electronic payments system. The yellow brick road which leads to profitable and successful deployment of electronic payments systems is littered with the corpses of schemes that were more concerned with putting a technological innovation into practice than meeting the specific needs of the customers. Dare I say that you have been warned!

A word about terminology. As readers will see, one of my basic faiths is that electronic payments systems give smaller financial institutions a high level of opportunity to compete for customer attention in the market-place with their larger competitors. Not that this means that I am in any sense prejudiced in favour of smaller financial institutions against larger institutions, but I would certainly champion any institution, large or small, which was doing its utmost to introduce electronic payments systems which met customer needs. In any event, in a retail financial sector where, depending on the country in question, building societies, savings institutions and other types of retail financial institutions are all likely to be in competition with banks, the generic term 'bank' is hardly appropriate to describe all these competing institutions. Consequently, in this book I prefer the term 'financial institution', which the reader should take to encapsulate any organization which is in the business of managing retail accounts, and particularly accounts held by private individuals. However, I use the term 'bank' when the organization under discussion is clearly a bank, and also in the conventional term 'banking technology', which refers to technology which any financial institution might deploy. Similarly, the term 'banker' is taken to mean anyone involved in providing retail financial services, whether via a recognized bank or any other type of financial institution.

Organization of the book

I have aimed to organize the material in the book so that there is a logical progression from polemical views on electronic payments systems to a detailed examination of the systems themselves, and on to wider industry issues, including an overview of the extent to which electronic payments systems are deployed in Europe, the United Kingdom and the United States.

Chapter one explains the social relevance of these systems, and looks in general at the impact which they have made within the retail financial sector, particularly in the UK.

Chapter two is a detailed examination of the origin and nature of Automated Teller Machines (ATMs) and ATM networks. The chapter concludes with specific guidelines on how to win new customers with ATMs.

Chapter three surveys EFTPoS, a major electronic payment system. This chapter also concludes with guidelines on winning new customers.

Chapter four looks at telephone banking, an important and rapidly growing sector; and provides guidelines on using telephone banking to win new customers.

Chapter five considers to what extent nascent smart card technology may impact on retail financial institutions during the next decade.

Chapter six is a step-by-step guide, from initial planning through implementation and post-implementation, to deploying an electronic payments system. The chapter concludes with a summary of the principal steps in the process.

Chapter seven surveys the implementation of electronic payments systems in the UK, US and continental Europe (Belgium, France, Germany, Italy, Luxembourg, The Netherlands, Portugal, Spain).

Chapter eight is a discussion of electronic payments systems from the customer's point of view.

Chapter nine is a summary of the likely future of electronic payment systems throughout the developed world.

The book concludes with a Glossary and Index.

CHAPTER ONE

The genesis of electronic payment systems

WHY DEPLOY ELECTRONIC PAYMENT SYSTEMS?

Electronic payment systems originated because the general public wanted a more convenient and rapid means of accessing their bank accounts. Financial institutions, in town, wanted to meet this need. With electronic payment systems, as with all aspects of banking technology, one sees the need driving the technological implementation, not vice versa.

While realizing that it is in their interests to meet customers' requirements, financial institutions have often tended to see the provision of electronic payment systems as a necessary evil, a chore, something that requires a high capital expense.

Slowly, however, the more perceptive institutions have come to realize that what was once a necessary evil could, if the deployment was properly managed and the benefits of the deployment properly communicated to customers, become a means for the institution to save money, provide an aggressive and positive level of service, and – most importantly of all – gain higher profits by winning new customers. This conceptual progression is the hub of the philosophy behind deploying electronic payment systems today.

Or at least it should be. All too often it isn't. Frequently, the scale of the task involved stifles the fresh, crystal-clear concepts which led to the desire to deploy the electronic payment system. If this process of stifling is happening in your institution, if you feel that the basic thinking behind the deploy-

ment of electronic payment systems is being eroded by committees, procedures and sheer volume of work, you may find it
useful to step back from the concerns of the day and consider
the relation between the development of electronic payment
systems over the past twenty years or so and the profound
changes in society which have occurred during that period.

ELECTRONIC PAYMENT SYSTEMS AND SOCIETY

I am not a social historian, nor an economist, but it does seem
reasonable to suggest that anyone seeking to make their career
in providing financial services to the general public ought to
be aware of the major social and historical trends which have,
over the decades, shaped the desires, aspirations and dreams
of that public. It is this public, after all, which constitutes the
market-place for financial services. I also believe that post-war
throughout the US and western Europe (and eastern Europe
too, albeit in a more restrained form) towards greater affluence,
more widespread ownership of the nation's assets and a
greatly increased desire on the part of individuals to have full
control of their finances and personal banking services, has
shaped the destiny and motivation of Americans and Europeans in a manner that financial institutions seeking retail
business ignore at their peril.

No one can contest that technology has played a huge role,
across many sectors other than just the provision of financial
services, in meeting the changing needs of the post-war public.
It is useful to consider banking technology as one part of the
entire take-up of technology by the public, since regarding
banking technology in this light emphasizes that new technology must always be subservient to public needs.

This attitude towards technology is a comparatively recent
one. Before, during and immediately after the Second World
War, many writers and other commentators, when considering
the likely role of technology in the future, were convinced that
technology would be a source of oppression to mankind, rather
than a source of liberation. E. M. Forster's pre-war short story

The Machine Stops, for example, presents a terrifying picture – admittedly in fairly naïve technological terms – of a future world where technology has so insulated people from the world that their muscles have started to atrophy, and their duties in serving 'the Machine' leave them little or no time to spend with loved ones. Aldous Huxley's bizarre novel *Brave New World* sees future society as essentially one large mass-production plant, with babies being behaviourally conditioned, after birth, to fit into strict categorizations of intellect, and with the influence of the world's first mass producer, Henry Ford, so pervasive that the year is no longer referred to in terms of Anno Domini but in terms of After Ford.

Nineteen Eighty-Four

The critique of technology *par excellence*, however, is George Orwell's *Nineteen Eighty-Four*. This was written in 1948 and Orwell wanted to name the book after the year in which it was written, but was persuaded to give it a futuristic date by his publishers. Now that we have passed 1984, it is easier to see the book less as a truly reliable forecast of the future but more as a cynical, despairing creation of a world where the privations of wartime Britain are continued forever. Nonetheless, *Nineteen Eighty-Four* became deservedly recognized as a brilliant warning about how human life could be shrunken and constricted by the dark influence of technology operated by a malevolent central government. Orwell's knowledge of technology was, like most novelists', somewhat scanty (for example, there are no references to computers in his book, although by 1948 electromechanical and electronic computers were already well established), but what is remarkable about the novel is that Orwell seems to take it for granted that technology can bring nothing but misery to the human race. Orwell was one of the most perceptive writers of his generation, but he appears unable to imagine any alternative scenario.

One man who was much influenced by reading *Nineteen*

Eighty-Four was Rob Farbrother, a former Operations Director of Citibank who, in 1985, formed Funds Transfer Sharing (FTS), a consortium of financial institutions wishing to benefit from participating in a shared Automated Teller Machine (ATM) network. In 1989 FTS underwent a management buyout (with several former FTS consortium members investing in the buy-out) and FTS became Nexus Payment Systems International, which has established a successful track record in marketing a wide range of electronic payment services to customers worldwide.

It may or may not be significant that Farbrother was born in 1948. At any rate, *Nineteen Eighty-Four* had a seminal influence on Farbrother's thinking when he read it in the 1960s. As he says:

> The book had an effect on me which I am sure Orwell did not intend his readers to draw. I saw in *Nineteen Eighty-Four* a vision of a society where automation played a crucial role. I decided then that I wanted to become a part of that automation, rather than a victim of it. But I did not want that automation to be oppressive. I felt very strongly that if the right people were in charge of the automation process, automation might be a benefit to mankind, rather than a form of oppression.

Farbrother's comment might seem a somewhat unsophisticated response to *Nineteen Eighty-Four*, yet when the year 1984 arrived, the simple fact was that Orwell's vision of a nightmarish, bleak future was unfulfilled, whereas the process of automation of society had progressed to levels that not even Orwell, for all his prescience in prophesizing the importance of technology in the future, had foreseen. Moreover, Farbrother had begun to play what has since turned out to be an important role in bringing the benefits of technology – rather than technological oppression – to the general public in several countries. He adds:

> In general, I feel that too many would be prophets experi-

ence a failure of imagination regarding technology, and always automatically assume that technology – at least in the future – will be hell-bent on dominating mankind and subjugating the human race to endless ages of oppression.

TECHNOLOGY AND THE CONSUMER

There is no doubt that prophets who think that technology will dominate mankind have got it wrong. In fact, experience shows that just as technology which does not meet real human needs is soon forgotten (do you remember 3D cinema or giant flying-boats?), electronic payment systems which do not win public approval soon fall into disuse. There is no avoiding the axiom that mankind is not a servant of technology; technology is a servant of man. Nor, indeed, would any reasonable person want this axiom to be otherwise.

Nonetheless, it is important for anybody involved in deploying technology within the retail financial sector to accept that among the general public there is, and will presumably continue to be, a wariness – even a fear – that the 'visible' technology used to operate electronic payment systems is somehow intimidating and threatening. This is in many ways a shame, because the last thing that the wise exponent of electronic payment systems wants is that customers pay more attention to the computer itself than to what the computer does. Only boffins are really interested in computers other than in terms of the applications that the computers can carry out. **Computers, in themselves, are not very important**. This might seem an odd thing for someone who writes about computers for a living to say, but it is true. Focusing on the computer at the expense of the application is dangerous, and all too likely to lead to the kind of unrealistic and mistaken thinking that invariably springs from implementing technology for technology's sake, rather than because the application is going to prove both a useful innovation and acceptable in the marketplace. It can hardly be emphasized enough that in the electronic payment system business, computers are a means to an end, and not the end itself.

After all, **consumers want solutions, not technology**. Rather than start out with the implicit attitude: 'This is the technology that I have, how can I present it to my consumers?', it is far better – indeed it is the only truly viable approach – to say, in effect, 'What do my consumers want and how can I deploy technology which meets those requirements?'

Some understanding of the particular nature of the problems presented by designing user interfaces for computer-driven systems is useful for anyone interested in deploying electronic payment systems to maximum competitive advantage. While the theory and practice of this subject requires a book to itself (I suggest two books on this subject in the bibliography), it is important to note here that all user interface designers who work with electronic payment systems agree that the computer element of the system should as far as possible be invisible: in other words, the user should not be aware that the computer is there. All that need concern the user is that he or she is obtaining from the payment system what he or she wants. As one book on this subject puts it:

> The user interface is the only possible way that the user can communicate with the computer. Quite unlike such an action as opening a door or wielding a stick, nothing the computer user does will produce an automatic and direct effect upon the computer. Every single aspect of the user's control over the computer must be built into the user interface. It follows, naturally, that the physical controls – such as a keypad, keyboard, joystick or mouse – which constitute the hardware of a computer user interface system, can only be symbolic aids to helping the user manipulate an action to which he has no real access, in the same way that a criminal trial is a symbolic way of re-enacting a crime which can never be re-enacted realistically. The greatest user design demands of all must be placed upon the designer of a human–computer interface, as the user will have nothing to start with, no obvious

handle or control which is suggested by the very nature of the tool. Even those familiar hardware elements of a computer, such as a keypad, keyboard, joystick or mouse, are used simply because they have been found to be convenient and ingenious ways for making the user feel that the computer is a physical tool like a hammer or a screwdriver, which it is not.*

This passage gives some idea of the user interface-related challenges that face anyone designing an interface for an electronic payment system, or indeed for any computer system. However, long before the user interface designers start making sense of the application, it is necessary to examine the type of requirements which consumers have from electronic payment systems. Of course, consumers would not quite see it in this way, since what they have are not requirements from an electronic payment system as such, but requirements from the financial institution which is currently handling their personal bank account, and which may carry out the same function tomorrow, too, if the institution continues to attract the customer's business.

HOW ELECTRONIC PAYMENT SYSTEMS ADDRESS CONSUMERS' BANKING REQUIREMENTS

So how do electronic payment systems meet the needs of financial institutions' customers? In order to understand this, it is first useful to analyse the needs that consumers have in terms of day-to-day banking. These needs may be seen as fitting into two principal categories.

1. **The consumer's need for account-related information.**
   First and foremost, consumers need information about the state of their account or accounts. The more up-to-date this information is the better, which is why the ideal situation

*Hicks, Richard and Essinger, James (1990) *Making Computers More Human – Designing for human-computer interface*, Elsevier, Oxford, p. 45.

is for account information to be provided on a real-time basis, that is, continually updated, with the latest updates being instantaneously available. A principal hazard of not providing real time information is that a consumer may act on earlier information which shows that he or she has sufficient funds available to complete a transaction, and then suffer the embarrassment – perhaps in a supermarket check-out queue – of being unable to proceed with the transaction. The need to take every reasonable measure to avoid any such embarrassment of a customer acting in good faith should be at the heart of any electronic payment system.

2. **The consumers' need for access to payment facilities**.

By definition, an electronic payment system is a computer-based system designed to allow the user rapid access to payment facilities. Obtaining access to these payment facilities is the next most important requirement of a customer. We can see the consumer's need for access to cash via the system as a specialized subset of the need for access to payment facilities, since in a cash withdrawal situation what is happening, in essence, is that the consumer is making a payment to himself or herself.

Generally speaking, and with the provisos that the making of the transactions must take place with maximum speed and privacy and that security measures are in place to ensure that only authorized persons make payment transactions, *any payment systems innovation which allows consumers to facilitate the obtaining of account-related information and/or the making of payments – whether by broadening the range of organizations to which payments may be made, or extending the facilities for making those payments – must be seen as representing a useful innovation.* By 'broadening the range of organizations to which payments may be made' I mean, for example, that a particular retail chain becomes able to accept a debit card which was not accepted before. By 'extending the facilities for making those payments' I mean, for example, the transition from the original obligation for customers to visit a branch of their financial institution during office hours to a way of making transactions out of office hours by means of an automated teller machine (ATM) or a telephone banking facility which allows payments to be made in the comfort of the account holder's own home.

The two types of consumer requirements mentioned above look straightforward, and they are. However, many practitioners of implementing electronic payment systems have found these requirements to furnish a career's worth of personal challenges.

CASE STUDY ONE   THE EVOLUTION OF LINK AND FUNDS TRANSFER SHARING

It was during Rob Farbrother's time at Citibank that the process began which led to him participating in the formation of the national shared ATM network LINK, and the independent consortium FTS. In 1984, seeing the huge lead which the leading UK clearing banks had established over it as providers of retail financial services, Citibank made a policy decision to help organize a network of retail financial institutions who were also anxious to gain a maximum competitive impetus over the largest clearers. Citibank's idea was to be an integral part of a network of institutions which could take advantage of the latest developments in electronic payment systems in order to compete, as far as possible, with the established clearers. At the time, there was a very real fear at Citibank (and in many other institutions) that if they did not act at once to exploit the opportunities presented by those latest technology, they ran the risk of being swamped by the large institutions and losing forever the ability to maintain a viable competitive presence in the UK market for retail financial services.

Certainly, the large clearing banks had already seen to it that they enjoyed what was in essence a 'built-in' advantage over their second rung rivals. For example, if an account holder had his or her salary paid in by an employer into an account at a clearing bank the money would be in the account on pay-day. If, on the other hand, the salary was paid into a building society, it would not be there until two days later. Further-more, by the early-1980s the large UK clearers had already begun creating networks of ATMs and were also beginning to start thinking about Electronic Funds Transfer at Point of Sale (EFTPoS). Without appearing to become too excited by it, the clearers had started to realize that by making use of electronic payment systems, and by exploiting their own membership of the Bankers Automated Clearing System (BACS) – which allowed the most rapid funds transfer – they could entrench themselves in privileged competitive positions from which they might never be dislodged.

However, one of the great advantages of technology is that it is available to everybody. Farbrother and some of his Citibank colleagues came fervently to believe that payment systems technology offered a huge potential for smaller financial insti-tutions – including even the smallest ones – to compete with their giant rivals.

If these small institutions could join forces and set up technological infrastructures which they could share with each other, there was every reason to think that they could offer their own customers a comparable – and perhaps even superior – level of service to that provided by the large clearers.

The political and regulatory climate in the UK was also right for the development of new, technology-based infrastructures within the retail banking sector. In the 1983 UK general election the ruling Conservative Government had been given a strong mandate by voters and the Government intended to use this mandate to reform the financial services sector; a sector which was generally regarded as being based too much on outdated traditional practices, some of which appeared even to restrict new entry and inhibit trade. This thinking on the part of the Government was to have its most explosive expression in the 1986 'Big Bang' and the passage of the Financial Services Act in the same year. However, the retail financial service sector was also coming under Government scrutiny. In particular, the UK building societies, which had always had the greatest aggregate share of the UK savings cake, but which had always been encumbered by regulations that confined them essentially to a role as savings institutions and mortgage lenders, were clearly regarded by the Government as representing a vast reserve of competitive strength.

Following the publication of the 1985 Childs Report,* the Building Societies Act of 1986 cleared away forever the rubble of the notion that the building societies were still little more than associations of sober self-improving Victorian artisans, and gave the societies the right to act as banks in all but name (and the right actually to become banks, a privilege of which the Abbey National later availed itself).

By the time the Building Societies Act was passed, Farbrother had not only played a key role in founding the consortium of which Citibank was a member, but he had been invited to work for the consortium full-time as its Managing Director. While at Citibank, as Chairman of the former ATM evaluation team, one of the conclusions which Farbrother had helped to formulate was the belief that the most productive and profitable deployment of ATMs was likely to stem from deploying them as consumer-oriented facilities and not as technological innovations for their own sake. Farbrother and his team based this conclusion around their own intuitive thinking and also on observations such as that the first ATM deployed in the US which achieved a success during the 1970s in terms of consumer transactions was called 'Tilly the Teller'.

As Farbrother points out:

> In the US, ATMs have from the beginning been 'humanized', with the result that the shared ATM networks in the USA go by weird and wonderful brand names ('Magic Line' is one that springs to mind). However, the need for orienting ATMs around consumers was only belatedly recognized in the UK. The UK clearers which first began

---

*The 1985 Childs Report recommended sweeping measures to give the UK building societies the opportunity to run accounts offering a full range of banking services.

deploying ATMs in the mid- to late-1970s made no comparable effort to 'humanize' their networks, but branded them rather unimaginatively with the name of the relevant bank, and then perhaps with the word 'cash' added. The idea that ATMs were a completely new delivery service offering hugely exciting marketing opportunities and the potential to provide what could be a seven-days-a-week, twenty-four hour service, appears, at least in the 1970s, not to have occurred to the big banks at all. Of course, the reasons were not hard to find. The big clearers were sure that they were the leading providers of retail financial services in the UK. This being the case, they did not see why they had any special cause to explore in depth the potential which ATMs offered as competitive weapons. Looking back, I realize that one reason why FTS was able to move ahead so quickly on the electronic payments front, and why, by 1986, we were already well on the way to deploying electronic payment systems that represented a formidable competitive challenge, was that we had understood that electronic payment systems were as much marketing tools as delivery tools, and above all had to be directed around winning acceptance among consumers. Which meant, in specific terms, that our ATMs were open for more hours in the day and for more days in the week than the big clearers' ATMs, and provided a wider range of services than theirs provided.

There was certainly no shortage of motivation for the FTS consortium to try to compete with the big clearers at winning new customers. Not all the consortium members were small institutions – Citibank certainly was not – but what they had in common was that they all craved a bigger share of the UK retail banking scene. Most of the consortium members had asked the big clearers whether they could join their networks and had encountered ignominious refusals. For the challengers, it was not enough merely to provide account facilities and a general level of service that was as good as the big clearers. They wanted to be better.

While working on founding FTS, Farbrother was also involved in helping to prepare a business plan for the funding and formation of the UK's first ever shared ATM network which would be aimed at the larger building societies who wanted to play more of a political role in the formation of the shared ATM network. This network was on-stream by 1986, and was known as LINK. FTS members entered LINK via FTS.

The creators of both LINK and FTS shared the vision of founding an infrastructure which would enable a member institution and their account holders to obtain access to the benefits offered by electronic payment systems (initially via a comprehensive and multi-function shared ATM facility), while at the same time keeping the expense of deploying the technology reasonable and proportionate to the financial institution's ability to pay. The financial benefits would stem directly from the simple fact that the system would be shared by numerous institutions, which would reap the benefits offered by economies of scale.

Above all, the beneficiary of the new system would be the customer, who would be able to gain access to an increasingly extensive shared national ATM network via financial institutions which had not been able to provide that service before the creation of FTS and LINK because they did not have a sufficiently large share of the market to justify the very high capital costs of setting up their own, dedicated, ATM network.

CASE STUDY TWO   THE HALIFAX BUILDING SOCIETY AND ITS
CARDCASH SYSTEM

Ironically, perhaps, in view of the fact that many of the principal UK beneficiaries of the mid-1980s surge in electronic payment systems were the customers of smaller institutions, a UK financial institution which launched one of the most successful ATM-centred retail banking accounts was the Halifax Building Society – the largest building society in the UK – which launched its CardCash account in 1984, and which until 1988 remained stubbornly independent of FTS; the national shared

ATM network LINK (of which FTS was a founding member and the conduit to LINK for FTS members) and the network MATRIX, a former rival to LINK which was aimed only at building societies.

At the same time as LINK and FTS were proving the great advantages electronic payment systems offered in terms of winning new customers and greatly broadening the width of the service being offered to existing customers, the Halifax Building Society was creating its own network of ATMs which would form the basis of CardCash: the first UK personal banking account which was designed to be, first and foremost, an ATM-based account. Card holders could use their cards inside branches if they wished, but there was no necessary need to go into the branch. The CardCash account was a great success for the Halifax, which enjoyed four years of steadily increasing numbers of CardCash card holders before deciding, in 1988, that it had extracted the maximum competitive advantage from the account that it could expect to extract, and was now willing to connect to LINK. By the time this happened LINK and MATRIX had merged, and LINK had achieved the vision of its founders: to create a national, multi-function, seven-day, twenty-four-hour shared network which would greatly increase members' abilities to compete with the major clearing banks.

THE EVOLUTION OF ELECTRONIC PAYMENT SYSTEMS

This chapter concludes with an extremely important theory which provides a convenient yardstick for assessing the stage of evolution, and indeed the likely ultimate prospects for the success of, any electronic payment system under consideration.

The theory states that there are three phases of evolution of an electronic payment system and that it is essential for any institution seeking to deploy the payment system in question to be aware exactly of which evolutionary phase the system occupies at any one time. According to this theory, the three evolutionary phases are the inception phase, the growth phase, and the maturity phase. It is important to note that the particular phase which applies to a payment system at any one time will depend within which country the payment system is being deployed since payment systems evolve at different rates in different countries. For example, smart cards are in a growth phase in France, which has proved itself a pioneer in smart card applications, but are very much at an inception stage in the UK, as indeed they are in most other countries.

Broadly speaking, the three phases of inception, growth and maturity relate, respectively, to:

- **inception**: the initial development of the technology and the ironing out of problems;
- **growth**: the period during which the effectiveness of the technology in the market-place is proven;
- **maturity**: the period of acceptance of the technology and widespread use by financial institutions and their customers. In the maturity phase, it can be expected that if an institution does not deploy the technology, it is likely to be at a serious competitive disadvantage to rival institutions.

More specifically, the characteristics of each evolutionary phase are described below.

The Inception Phase

The characteristics of this phase are:

- the technology is still being developed and technical problems remain to be ironed out;
- the technology is not widely available commercially;
- substantial investment will be required by any bank which seeks to develop technology which is currently in this phase; this would generally preclude the development by any but the largest bank or computer systems house;
- an element of risk is inherent in the development – this can hardly be avoided, since ultimately the bank has no way of being certain that the technology in question will

prove acceptable to the bank's retail customers (in the case of a technological development for retail banking) or will be found to be useful and profitable by the bank's staff.

In the UK, examples of payment systems which are currently in the inception phase are smart cards and personal computer-based home banking.

The Growth Phase

The characteristics of this phase are:

- the technology is widely available commercially;
- the technology is increasingly accepted by the people for whom it is intended;
- since much of the major development investment expenditure will have been made by the pioneer deployers, banks wishing to deploy this technology will probably not need to face high development costs;
- banks which do not deploy this technology will be under increasing competitive pressure;
- there is a distinct tendency towards increased deployment of the technology;
- the technology has not yet reached a point where the majority of banks provide it.

Although the last two characteristics may appear contradictory this is not the case since the overriding characteristic of the growth phase is that implementation of the technology is in a state of dynamic change, with more and more banks becoming interested in deploying the technology, although saturation point is still several years away.

Several types of payment systems – including EFTPoS and telephone banking – are in the growth phase in most countries.

The Maturity Phase

The characteristics of this phase are:

- the technology is now being used by most, if not all, banks;

◆ there is widespread acceptance of the technology among the people for whom it is intended;
◆ banks are now generally expected by consumers to have the technology and those which do not have it available are consequently likely to be at a severe competitive disadvantage;
◆ further gains in competitive advantage can only be made in providing refinements of the technology.

A principal type of banking technology in the maturity phase within the UK banking scenario is the ATM. ATMs are so widespread among the UK banking community that the majority of customers probably use an ATM more often than they visit a bank branch. Since this is the case, the deployment of ATMs itself probably no longer confers a competitive advantage on a bank, as the bank's customers expect the bank to have this facility. However, there is still scope for banks to gain a competitive advantage from their ATM deployment by adding additional features – such as payment to third parties and other retail services – to their ATMs. Another possibility is for the bank to join a shared ATM network which will offer, in effect, a much larger number of ATMs to the bank's customers, and may also open up possibilities for international sharing, with the result that a UK bank's customers could withdraw cash (in local currency) from an overseas ATM.

ELECTRONIC PAYMENT SYSTEMS AS A MARKETING TOOL

That the progression of the different types of payment system through the three phases outlined is a reasonably steady one should not obscure the fact that financial institutions can never be complacent about how the market-place will react to a new form of payment system. The types of payment systems mentioned in the analysis of the three phases are all tried and tested types, which have been found to offer important possibilities for wide customer acceptance.

Even more important, the types of electronic payment

system mentioned have demonstrated actual, or potential, benefit to financial institutions as **marketing tools**; that is, methods by which customers can not only receive the institution's services but also are so impressed by the usefulness of the system that they are likely to use the service more often, or even to encourage their friends and relatives to use it. This, in essence, is the point at which an electronic payment system starts to help an institution to win new customers. What more could an institution want from a new type of technology?

Nonetheless, the payment system depends for its success or public acceptance. Technological developments create opportunities for, but do not guarantee, successful deployment. A successful deployment is most likely to stem from a correct estimate (ideally based on market research) of what the customer actually wants from his or her financial institution, with the payment system then being tailored to meet those requirements as precisely as possible. Since matching an electronic payment system to these requirements is of the utmost importance, this book devotes an entire chapter (Chapter Six) to this subject.

Even where an in-depth investigation has been mounted of consumers' needs and requirements, a basic fear of using the new technology may, as mentioned above, afflict users, particularly the elderly. This fear – which might be termed 'techno-fear' – must be rigorously dealt with by the institution. One way of combating a fear of ATMs, for example, would be to give a new customer a cheque for £1, and tell them that if they can deposit it in an ATM, it's theirs. Simplistic this example might be, but it helps to show yet again the importance of an institution bearing in mind the market-place acceptability, or otherwise, of a payment system at every stage of its deployment.

Financial institutions must never allow themselves to start thinking that there is a clear equation between ingenuity of technological development and acceptability in the market-place. No such equation exists.

A crucial test of market-place acceptability of a new form of payment system comes when the technology is in any sense a pioneering one. In the past, financial institutions have sometimes deployed a pioneering technology with more thought for the fact that it is a pioneering technology than that it will be widely accepted. All too often such thinking leads to disaster. The golden rule is: *if you don't know that the application will be viable, be cautious about over-hasty deployment of it, however clever and innovative the technology seems to be*. The market-place does not care about the innovatory nature of a particular technology but only about the benefits which it is going to offer. It is dangerous and potentially very costly for an institution to adopt the attitude that it ought to deploy technology for technology's sake.

Fortunately, the retail financial services sector now boasts very many talented people who are responsible for specifying new types of electronic payment systems, and the unrestrained deployment of technology for its own sake, rather than because the technology will benefit users, is something that is seen with increasing rarity. Nonetheless, there is always a danger that it will again rear its head, particularly where the information technology director or systems manager in question has a background in computing rather than in banking. It is for this, and other reasons, that the most successful deployments of electronic payment systems on today's financial services sector are achieved by teams led by people who are bankers first and foremost, and only secondarily technologists.

CHAPTER TWO

Automated Teller Machines

THE NATURE OF ATMS

Automated Teller Machines (ATMs) are automatic machines for dispensing banking services to customers. They are the most immediately visible type of retail banking technology and can be seen as the most important electronic payment system. As payment system devices, they have two main applications.

1. Customers can withdraw cash from them and so in effect can make themselves the recipient of the payment service.
2. Many financial institutions enable customers to initiate payments to third parties via ATMs.

Worldwide, ATMs play a key role in the efforts of most retail banks to win business from consumers. Already, many institutions' customers see ATMs as a more typical interface between themselves and their retail financial institution than the institution's branch.

There are two principal types of ATMs: **through-the-wall (TTW) ATMs**, which are located in the outside wall of a branch of a financial institution and which should ideally be available for use round the clock; and **lobby ATMs**, which are either located inside a financial institution's branch or in some other place (e.g. a supermarket) where there is likely to be a substantial demand for cash. Many lobby ATMs situated in branches are dedicated to particular functions, e.g. deposit making, statement ordering, etc.

All ATMs have some kind of link with the central computer of the institution that operates them. Where this link takes place in **real-time**, the link is simultaneous with the ATM being operated by the card holder. Where **batch processing** is used, the ATM connects only to the central computer at certain times of the day, in order to relay details of completed transactions.

The question of whether an ATM operates in real-time or by means of batch processing affects two important factors relating to the system as follows.

1. **The breadth of the range of services available to customers**
   Since a real-time system connects directly and simultaneously to the computer which holds details of the card holder's account, an ATM operating in real-time can provide a wider and more up-to-date range of account information than an ATM which does not have this facility.

2. **The security of the system**
   ATM transactions are almost universally authorized by means of the card holder tapping a memorized Personal Identification Number (PIN) into the ATM's console. Real-time systems are more secure than batch-processing systems because they can check the PIN against details held invisibly within the central computer. There is no danger that the card holder will draw more funds out of the account than are available because each request for withdrawal can easily be checked against the card holder's account details. Where batch processing is used, not only must the PIN be held in encrypted form within the magnetic stripe on the card but the institution must restrict withdrawals to a certain daily limit. There is the danger that the card could be copied by unscrupulous persons and that numerous withdrawals could be made against the daily limit for withdrawal to which each card holder has access.

THE ORIGIN OF ATMS

ATMs originated in the US during the late 1960s. The credit for developing ATM technology is usually accorded to the Texas corporation Docutel, a former subsidiary of Recognition Equipment. In the late 1960s, Docutel had tentatively identified a market for machines that would give bank customers access to their funds around the clock, seven days a week. At the time, Docutel was involved in other areas of activity, including automated baggage handling and automated petrol pumps. Following the identification of the new market sector, Docutel began to develop what it called the Automated Teller Machine: at that point rather an ambitious statement of the functions which the new devices would carry out, since initially the machines only dispensed cash.

In 1969 a venture capital consortium purchased Docutel from Recognition Equipment with a view to bringing ATMs into production without delay. The consortium's first ATMs were installed on Long Island, New York, by Chemical Bank in 1969. The idea caught on quickly and Docutel prospered. By 1974 the company had acquired a 70% share of the US ATM market.

The year 1974, while marking a high point for Docutel, was also the beginning of the end for the corporation. A worldwide recession bit into the profits of financial institutions, which also lost money in the slump in real estate values. In 1974, and during the following two years, few institutions had the money to buy ATMs. Docutel was making good machines but the market could not afford to take them. Docutel's problems were compounded by the fact that the corporation did not have any business areas where it could maintain profits while the recession continued.

Even given the need for financial restraints, US banks were at the time displaying considerable conservatism in their approach to ATMs. Although they had begun to see the advantages of the new machines, they were initially not particularly willing to issue debit cards (i.e. cards which access a current account or savings account, as opposed to credit cards which access a credit line or credit facility) for use in conjunction with

ATMs. The main reason was that they feared that issuing these cards would create security problems. In particular, US banks did not want to provide the cards to people who were not creditworthy. As a result, initially only credit card holders were allowed to use the new machines.

US BANKS' FAILURE OF IMAGINATION

The story of the early days of ATMs is a good example of how some financial institutions have sufficient **technological imagination**, but insufficient **market-place imagination**. By this I mean that an institution is able to see how new technology might be deployed, but is not able to grasp the full implications of what deployment might mean for it in terms of increased appeal to the consumer and enhanced market share. In the case of the US institutions which pioneered ATMs, the conservative strategy which they applied to the business of distributing the debit cards did not take full advantage of the new invention and failed to give the benefits of ATMs to the very people who needed them.

BRINGING ATMS TO THE PEOPLE

Who were these people who needed ATMs? Not only white-collar workers, who could very often visit branches of financial institutions during lunch-breaks or at other times, since they tended to work in offices located near enough to the branches. It was blue-collar workers and manual workers who had the most to gain from ATMs. Very often, working in plants and factories located away from town centres, they had little or no opportunity to visit a branch during the day and so were restricted to doing their banking transactions on Saturday morning (assuming that the branch was open on Saturday morning), or else have somebody else visit the branch on their behalf. An ATM, however, which was operating in the evenings and throughout weekends, could represent a good solution to this problem. Unfortunately, however, the failure of institutions' technological imaginations was to persist for some time yet. Only when institutions had the conviction and courage to allow more people to use ATMs could the machines generate the transaction volumes that would justify their installation. As late as 1974, the highest volume ATM in downtown Chicago processed only 2000 transactions a month. This compared unfavourably with the 4000 monthly transactions that the average human bank teller dealt with at this time.

BANKS' FAILURE TO UNDERSTAND THE COMPETITIVE POWER OF ATMS

Equally, the possibilities which ATMs offered institutions that deployed them to establish a competitive advantage over institutions had as yet hardly been factored into the thinking. In those early days, ATMs were simply seen as a means to reduce pressure on cashiers, principally by mechanizing the cash dispensing function.

PROVING THE USEFULNESS OF ATMS

Appropriately enough, one of the last acts of ATM pioneer Docutel as an independent corporation was to prove to US banks that ATMs could greatly exceed human tellers in terms of transaction volume. In 1974, displaying characteristic courage despite the world banking recession, Docutel installed 'Tilly the Teller' at First Atlanta Bank, Atlanta, Georgia. Tilly was the first of many attempts in the US to give ATMs a 'human' or 'user-friendly' branding. It is also interesting to note that Tilly was much more than a mere cash dispenser: it allowed customers to check their balances, pay bills, make deposits and transfer funds between different accounts. For the first time, the term 'Automated Teller Machine' was an appropriate description of what the machine actually did. Tilly was successful, soon establishing a monthly volume of around

10 000 transactions, which is on a par with the monthly volumes of many ATMs in capital cities today.

THE DEMISE OF DOCUTEL

However, for all the success of Tilly and similar machines supplied by Docutel, the pioneer's days were drawing to a close. By 1976 it was clear that Docutel had lost its lead as chief ATM manufacturer in the US to IBM and Diebold, both of which had the resources to survive the difficult years of the mid-1970s. Docutel thus became number three rather than number one. Nor was the ATM pioneer well placed for the next stage of the competition, which involved the refinement of ATM technology. In this new scenario of things, it was the electronics corporations with the most cash available for research into associated electronic issues which were likely to achieve the greatest success in the ATM stakes.

During the late 1970s Docutel began to move away from ATMs, as the corporation sought other types of equipment for its salespersons to sell, including more familiar office equipment. Docutel later merged with Olivetti.

CURRENT MAJOR MANUFACTURERS OF ATMS

Nowadays, the world's largest manufacturer of ATMs is NCR, which produces about 10 000 ATMs annually at its plant in Dundee, Scotland. NCR began producing ATMs in the early 1970s and supplies the machines to financial institutions worldwide. Like IBM and Diebold, NCR was able to apply resources, and expertise that it had gained from successful operation in other business machinery fields, to the problem of supplying ATMs. From the outset NCR's ATMs have offered a highly competitive edge in terms of offering the latest ATM functions to financial institutions and their customers.

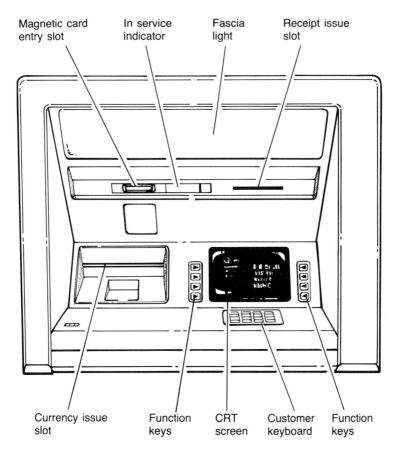

Magnetic card entry slot

In service indicator

Fascia light

Receipt issue slot

Currency issue slot

Function keys

CRT screen

Customer keyboard

Function keys

Fig. 2.1 Front configuration of a typical ATM. Source: NCR Ltd.

TECHNICAL ASPECTS OF ATMS

Figure 2.1 shows the front configuration of a typical ATM. Although different manufacturers' ATMs have different types of dashboards for the user interface, this figure illustrates the typical functions which are available on ATMs. This particular brand of machine also features a screen (not shown) which slides down to cover the front interface between transactions. However, not all ATMs have this feature.

Manufacturing and marketing ATMs ties up a good deal of capital, which is one reason why the world's major ATM manufacturers – IBM, NCR, Philips and Fujitsu – are all large organizations for which ATM manufacture is only a relatively small part of their total business activity. However, even organizations of this calibre cannot afford to waste money on building new types of ATMs which banks will not want to buy and customers will not wish to use. Manufacturers have to arrive at a careful balance between getting ahead of the competition by putting research cash into designing new ATM models, and the need for new developments to be acceptable to the market.

As we have seen, ATMs are generally sited in three types of location: in the outside wall of the branch (ATMs located here are generally known as 'through-the-wall ATMs'); in a third-party 'sheltered' location, such as in a supermarket or shopping mall; and in a vestibule – a special secluded room inside a financial institution's premises which is open 24 hours a day, or at least open more hours than the branch. Vestibules are important locations in cold countries and geographic regions such as Canada or Scandinavia, but are less important for the UK.

Although third-party and vestibule ATMs normally resemble standard through-the-wall machines, there are usually differences in design between lobby and through-the-wall ATMs. Some lobby ATMs, for instance, dispense balance information rather than cash, and so contain no built-in safes.

ATMS AS A COMPETITIVE WEAPON

In an increasingly competitive retail banking business, financial institutions are always on the lookout for ways of wooing new customers, keeping existing customers happy and, at the same time, cutting costs. In the UK, for example, the clearing banks and the building societies are competing with each other for the same customers; customers who, seeing how competitive the market-place is, are less likely to have a long standing loyalty to use one particular institution's services exclusively.

As the principal electronic payment system for any retail financial institution, ATMs can be said to be at the heart of the struggle to win customers. Highly visible, ATMs are already a feature of UK high streets and the next few years are likely to see their increased deployment in smaller towns, as well as in 'sheltered' locations.

ATM DEVELOPMENT IN THE FUTURE

Not surprisingly, ATM manufacturers – who wish to prevent their rivals from finding out anything about future plans – are not eager to reveal what they consider will be the most important future developments in ATM technology. However, research around the industry has highlighted some of the more significant advances in future ATM technology.

By far the most important imminent advance appears to be the use of colour graphics. The attraction of colour both to financial institutions and their customers makes it likely that colour will become a common feature of ATMs. However, current technology cannot provide colour screens with sufficient contrast to be used satisfactorily in outdoor locations, so at present colour screens can only be used with lobby, sheltered location or vestibule ATMs.

There is also abundant scope for further developments in the range of functions provided by ATMs. The most usual functions which can be accessed by ATMs are as follows:

◆ cash withdrawal;
◆ details of balance provided;
◆ statements ordered;
◆ deposit facility (but only via ATMs which are operated by the institution which holds the card holder's account);
◆ initiation of payments to third parties (assuming that details of payees have already been provided to the institution by the card holder);
◆ provision of travellers' cheques (worldwide, only American Express has made this a primary function of its ATMs).

Other functions are also becoming available in some countries and new ATMs often reflect these additional functions. NCR, for example, has added an 80-column statement printer function to some of its ATMs, and it already supplies some Spanish banks with ATMs which feature a passbook updating facility. In the UK, passbook updating is not an important function for banks, which do not tend to issue passbooks, but all UK building societies do, and passbook updating may become a common feature of British building society ATMs in the years to come.

Other additions to the range of ATM facilities which are currently under consideration, or likely to come under consideration in the near future, include: personal loan application and authorization; share purchase; analysis of and suggested modification in the card holder's personal investment portfolio; purchase of a wide range of tickets (in many countries, including the UK, buying railway tickets through ATMs is already possible via some specialized ATMs located in railway stations); and other types of ATM-related shopping. ATMs might even be used one day as constituents of specialized telecommunications networks, with card holders able to summon emergency medical or other types of help via the ATM.

THE CONCEPT OF NATIONAL ATM SHARING

The previous chapter looked at case studies which illustrated how organizations were formed to exploit the great benefits of national ATM sharing (i.e. ATM sharing within one country). It is widely accepted that the full benefits of ATMs will only be felt by institutions and their customers when the ATMs are involved in sharing arrangements with other institutions' machines. Since the ATM is a relatively expensive device and likely to stay that way for the foreseeable future, there is every incentive for financial institutions to share ATM networks with each other, thereby greatly reducing the cost of offering their customers access to a wide – even nationwide – network.

Overall, the principal advantages to a financial institution from participation in a nationally shared ATM network appear to be as follows.

◆ Financial constraints, a sheer limit on the number of branches which an institution operates or a combination of these factors, will in most cases restrict the number of ATMs which an institution could provide if operating the ATM network independently. ATM sharing will give the institution's customers access to a much greater number of ATMs, thereby making the institution's services more attractive to the consumer.

◆ The institution will consequently be able to make substantial cost savings compared with the cost of continually extending its ATM network on an independent basis.

◆ The institution will gain benefits in terms of market awareness as a result of the branding of the shared network.

◆ The shared network will probably have more financial resources and know-how available specifically for ATM deployment and associated research than an institution running a proprietary network could.

◆ By belonging to a shared network, the institution will gain access to such network benefits as international ATM sharing with overseas shared networks. It is unlikely that a bank would be able to obtain such benefits if it operated its network on an independent basis. International ATM sharing is considered in detail later in this chapter.

COMPETITIVE FACTORS MOTIVATING NATIONAL ATM SHARING

Apart from the realization on the part of institutions that ATM sharing offers such important benefits as the above, national ATM sharing has also been driven by the view that the competitive advantage of proprietary ATM networks had – by the early-1980s – been largely exhausted in most of the countries which had been deploying ATMs since the mid-1970s. Larger institutions sometimes prefer initially to set up their own proprietory network rather than share. However, once they feel that they have gained as much competitive benefit from deploying their own network as they can reasonably expect, they are usually only too willing to participate in a shared network.

If shared national ATM networks are to run amicably and successfully, all member institutions must have reason to be confident that their customers' information remains as confidential within the shared network as it would remain within the institution's own proprietary network. The shared network must be seen to function fairly and the network operator must run the network with equal concern for all the members of the network; including the smaller members who may well fear that their own interests will be swamped by larger members.

THE PARTICULAR BENEFITS TO SMALLER INSTITUTIONS OF ATM SHARING

A shared network's smaller member institutions are likely, in the short term, to obtain the greatest immediate benefits from participating in shared ATM networks. Such small institutions may only have resources for deploying a few ATMs of their own – and may indeed not be able to afford any ATMs of their own at all. For such smaller institutions, participation in a shared network can lead to a major extension of the institutions resources. However, in the medium- to long-term, all members of a shared ATM network will benefit considerably from their membership.

Ideally, a shared ATM network will allow all the ATMs on the network – whether or not owned by the customer's own institution – to provide the full range of transactions as soon as the ATMs are connected. The tendency today is for shared networks to strive for this ideal, with the only exception being that deposits are usually only accepted by ATMs operated by the customer's own institution, since the paperwork and security problems involved in clearing physical deposits of cash or cheques do not usually make the provision of the facility worthwhile.

MAKING SHARED NETWORK TECHNOLOGY SECURE

Today's switching technology allows transactions to be switched across the shared network with great facility and the technical management of a network presents no great problems apart from the need to ensure, both for shared and proprietary networks, that in the event of a major fire, power loss or other accident striking the network's computer centre, operational facilities are in place to ensure that the central computer facility can either continue its activities uninterrupted, or else continue activities with the absolute minimum of downtime. The best precaution against a complete systems failure is for an institution either to set up a duplicate central computer systems facility to which the system's activities can rapidly be transferred in an emergency, or for the institution to subscribe to what is usually known as a 'disaster recovery facility': that is, a facility which several institutions share and to which they would have immediate access if their system went down. Although the likelihood of two or more institutions suffering a systems failure at the same time is negligible, shared disaster recovery facilities should have a contingency plan for this eventuality, for example, by formulating a scheme which would provide for the other institutions in the scheme to help out with their own spare computer capacity. In the vast majority of cases, of course, the shared facility will only be needed by one institution at a time.

BASING NEW ACCOUNTS AROUND THE ATM NETWORK

A financial institution will only make the most of a commitment to an independent or shared ATM network if it launches new types of personal or corporate banking accounts which are closely based around the ATM. These accounts will enable the institution to exploit to the full the popularity of ATMs among customers, while also allowing customers to benefit from the increasingly wide range of functions that are becoming available via ATMs. In the UK, for example, building societies and other financial institutions which are not major clearing banks have shown a great willingness to make the most of the competitive advantages offered by ATMs and shared ATM networks by creating new types of account based upon the proprietory or shared ATM facility. The willingness of such institutions to do this generally exceeds that displayed by the main clearing banks.

ATM SHARING IN THE UK

In the UK the concept of shared ATM networks has been particularly wholeheartedly embraced by British building societies, which for historical reasons tend to have locally-orientated customer bases although some of the larger societies are already entirely national institutions. Indeed, such are the competitive advantages conferred by shared ATM networks that even the smallest UK building societies are able to offer their customers a nationwide ATM-based service network which competes on equal terms with the leading UK clearing banks' nationwide branch-based service network.

ATM SHARING IN THE US

In the US, where the shared ATM networks concept was pioneered, the networks have been even more successful than in the UK. The success of shared networks in the US has undoubtedly been spurred on by traditional US banking legislation, which generally restricts banks to operating within their locality. Most banks have no opportunity to offer their customers banking services on an interstate basis except by participating in a shared ATM network.

INTERNATIONAL ATM SHARING

A logical and exciting extension of the principal of national ATM sharing is that of international sharing, which involves a financial institution's ATM network being connected with the ATM network of one or more institutions located abroad. Although there is no reason why a single institution should not conclude an international sharing arrangement with a foreign institution, in practice international sharing tends to take place between shared ATM networks rather than between lone institutions.

The most obvious application and relevance of international sharing relates to meeting the cash needs of people travelling abroad. In this context, it is certainly relevant to point out that an increasing number of international travellers have already become accustomed to including plastic cards with their foreign currency and travellers cheques as part of their basic requirements for making payments overseas. During the late-1970s, travel and entertainment charge cards, such as American Express and Diners Club, became an important facility for the business traveller. In the 1980s, with the rapid growth of the Visa and Mastercard/Access networks – and, to a lesser degree, Eurocheque – the enactment of card-based international payments became feasible for much larger numbers of travellers, with private tourists standing to benefit from the facility as much as business travellers.

During the 1990s, one of the most significant developments in international card usage is likely to be in the sharing of ATM facilities between financial institutions and networks in different countries. Travellers using such facilities would be able to withdraw foreign currency cash, while abroad, from home-based accounts via an ATM, thus in theory obtaining the same level of convenience from ATMs that these machines provide on the high street at home. It is particularly important to bear in mind that the traveller need not always be limited to taking cash advances on credit and charge card accounts, since the lower cost option of debit/ATM cards is becoming more widely available.

Overall, what options are there for travellers who wish to obtain foreign currency? To some extent, the situation differs from country to country, but there is sufficient similarity between countries for the example of the UK to act as a reasonable generalization of the position in the industrialized countries. There is certainly no doubt that cash remains the dominant payment method in every country in the world. This is even true in a country, such as Japan, where credit cards are firmly established. Indeed, the Japanese tend not to make payments with cheques, but prefer cash.

In other words, any electronic payment system which is able to provide travellers with secure, rapid access to cash at the minimum cost ought to be highly successful.

CASE STUDY THREE   METHODS FOR A UK-BASED TRAVELLER TO OBTAIN FOREIGN CURRENCY

Firstly, the most obvious way for a UK-based traveller to obtain foreign currency is for him or her to buy it from a bank or building society at home. All high street banks, and some building societies, can arrange from foreign currency to be collected, subject to advance notice being given by the customer. Foreign currency must almost always be paid for in full on the date of collection and will be subject to commission charges. These typically amount to 1–2% of the amount of currency supplied, subject to a certain minimum commission and in some cases also to a maximum commission level.

Unfortunately, there are distinct disadvantages to the apparently simple procedure of ordering cash back home and taking it abroad. The most obvious problem is that the traveller is naturally fully liable in the event of the cash being lost, and would therefore be rather unwise to carry the full cash requirement for a long trip. Another problem is that the surplus cash that remains at the end of a trip will be subject to commission charges on being exchanged back into sterling. Coins often cannot be exchanged back at all. Needless to say, exchange rates will reflect a spread in buying or selling rates that favours the financial institution.

Secondly, the traveller may purchase travellers cheques. These certainly give the traveller the peace of mind and practical benefit of the prospects of a refund in the event of a loss, but they must be paid for in advance and can result in a substantial commission charge. On purchase 1–2% is usually levied to cover the 'insurance' element of the cheques and the administration charges of the financial institution. In addition, there will also be foreign exchange commission to pay in the UK if foreign currency cheques are purchased, or abroad if sterling travellers cheques are chosen. Even when the traveller opts for foreign currency cheques it is likely that the financial institution abroad will wish to levy additional commission for handling the cheques. Who, on buying travellers cheques and following the expensive encashment procedures, has not had the depressing feeling that the objective of travellers cheques is to deprive the traveller of his or her hard-earned holiday money?

Travellers cheques are, in most cases, easily encashed at banking branches during opening hours or at bureaux de change with extended opening hours. The latter are, however, likely to offer poor exchange rates combined with high commission charges (2% is not uncommon). Access to cash at weekends and bank holidays will be severely restricted. Major hotels are often able to cash travellers cheques (although some restrict this facility to hotel residents). However, hotels also tend to charge high commission, and besides, should a holiday-maker (or indeed a business person) have to restrict their overseas activity to being in the vicinity of large hotels?

A final drawback with travellers cheques – not often mentioned by the issuing organizations – is that there are definite restrictions on the acceptance of travellers cheques, in certain currencies, in many countries. Within eastern Europe and many parts of the Third World, for example, US dollar travellers cheques are greatly preferred to travellers cheques in other currencies – including sterling, and it is sometimes difficult to persuade banks to accept cheques in the other currencies.

A third option is for the traveller to use Eurocheques. In Europe, at least, these are widely accepted at banking branches and at bureaux de change. Local currency can be withdraw to a certain pre-set value of about £100. The Eurocheque cheque book, if issued specially, and Eurocheque ATM/cheque guarantee cards are subject to annual fees and, additionally, there is likely to be a 1.6% commission charge levied by the issuing bank, as well as handling charges of about thirty pence per debit. Eurocheques are therefore a relatively expensive option. However, the traveller benefits through not having to pay for the cash withdrawals before leaving the UK, and through the wide acceptability of Eurocheques in Europe.

Eurocheque has developed an extensive international ATM network of 25 000 ATMs supporting its 60 million card holders across Europe. A Eurocheque card holder with a Personal Identification Number (PIN) can access these ATMs for cash up to about £100 per withdrawal at approximately the same charges as levied for paper Eurocheques.

A fourth option is that of American Express or Diners Club charge cards. Although these are widely accepted for purchase abroad, they are less convenient for international cash advances than bank credit card brands, such as Visa. Both American Express and Diners Club are subject to a high annual fee. Cash advances are subject to a percentage fee: typically 1.5% for American Express or 4% for Diners Club. Bills are settled in the normal way at the end of the month. Card holders are expected to settle their bills promptly and in full, and are liable to have their charge facilities withdrawn if they do not do this. However, there is clearly the opportunity to obtain cash now and pay for it later, although relatively high fees must be paid for this privilege.

Another important drawback with charge cards is that, in the UK and Europe (less so in the US) these cards are only issued to people who are adjudged by the issuing organizations to be of a sound financial standing and to have a certain specified minimum income. This means that many people cannot obtain charge cards and therefore cannot obtain cash while abroad by this method.

The fifth option is credit cards, which are also only available to people who have been adjudged to have a requisite level of personal creditworthiness. The main credit cards issued in the UK are Visa and Mastercard/Access. These have a high worldwide acceptance, including a large number of banking branches and agencies through which cash can be withdrawn. There is a tendency for annual fees in the vicinity of about £10 to be levied by financial institutions issuing Visa and Mastercard/Access credit cards, although the levying of the fee is not yet universal among issuers.

Obtaining cash abroad on a credit card is expensive. Cash advances are subject to a percentage fee – normally 1.5% – and interest charges which apply **from the date of withdrawal** until settlement (in full) have the potential to cost another 2% per month. Policies on exchange rates vary considerably, but even though these are certainly better than those at bank branches and bureaux de change, a profit on the transaction of the institution is still, of course, factored into the rate.

Cash advances can be taken via ATMs if a PIN has been issued for the card but these will be subject to the standard cash advance charge. In fact, the majority of credit card holders, whatever country they originate from, are not aware of their PIN and of the locations where they can make international withdrawals. This has much to do with most travellers being relatively unfamiliar with using their credit cards in ATMs to withdraw cash.

Table 2.1 summarizes the different charges for taking money abroad which are outlined above.

The final option open to travellers is to obtain cash via international ATM sharing using the same ATM card as issued locally, and with the same PIN. The advantages of travellers obtaining cash from ATMs operated by financial institutions that participate in a sharing arrangement with the traveller's own institutions back home are as described below.

ADVANTAGES TO TRAVELLERS OF OBTAINING CASH FROM ATMS ABROAD

1. Since the international agreement would almost certainly be between national shared networks, it is likely that the traveller will have access to a relatively large number of ATMs in the country within which he or she was travelling.

Table 2.1 Comparative costs of ways of travellers having access to cash abroad

Type	Typical customer charges			
	Commission	Annual card fee (£)	Enrolment (£)	Cheque (pence)
CR card cash advance	1.5% (+interest)	0–12	–	–
CR card cash disp.	1.5% (+interest)	0–12	–	–
Amex charge card cash disp.	1% (min £1)	32.50	–	–
Diners charge card cash disp.	Guideline: 1–4%	27.00	£20.00 pa	–
Eurocheque card	1.6%	5–6	–	30
Foreign currency	0.5–1% (min £1, max. £10)	–	–	–
Postcheques (Girobank)	1%	–	–	60
Sterling conversion abroad	1%+	–	–	–
Travellers cheque	1–1.5% (Sterling) 1.5–2% (Foreign) + commission when cashed	–	–	–

2. The arrangement would give the traveller direct access to his or her own personal account back home. No credit line or charge facility would need to be involved, so far more people could benefit from this facility than are able to benefit from using charge cards and credit cards abroad.

3. The very fact that ATMs are at the hub of the arrangement means that the traveller would have flexibility in terms of opening hours, including weekends and bank holidays.

4. The traveller could reasonably expect a favourable exchange rate, based on interbank rates.

5. The traveller would only need to settle transactions at the

moment when he or she actually makes the withdrawal – whether the withdrawal is actioned in real-time or a day or so later. This way, the traveller avoids the need for making advance payments (as with travellers cheques and with buying currency in advance).

6. The traveller would probably enjoy free card issue, without an annual fee.

7. The low cost, electronic nature of the transaction should allow the financial institution to charge the customer less than for other travel facilities, without jeopardizing the institution's profit margin.

8. The cash withdrawal is efficient and easy to perform according to principles identical to using an ATM at home and using the PIN with which the customer is familiar (i.e. not a special PIN, as with credit card-based withdrawals).

From the above it would appear that international ATM sharing is a near-ideal solution to the problem of providing financial institutions' customers with cash when abroad. However, one drawback to the system is that a customer is only going to use an international ATM facility as his main source of foreign currency when abroad if he is confident that the facility will give him the currency that he needs. Obviously, occasions when the international sharing arrangement is not functioning for any reason are likely to dent users' confidence. For the time being, until customers are very familiar with these arrangements and are confident that they can rely on the foreign ATMs to provide cash as and when required, travellers are likely to want to use alternative methods of having access to cash in addition to the ATM sharing facility. But, just as the use of national ATMs increased greatly once customers became familiar with the technology and were confident that the machines were reliable, we may reasonably expect international ATM sharing arrangements to become increasingly attractive to customers in the future.

In the immediate future, transaction volumes are unlikely to be very high. The added value to the card holders, however, will be considerable as a contingency fall-back and as a convenient means of obtaining money while travelling.

The potential market for international ATM sharing is the same as for other travel facilities and is naturally related to the amount of travel abroad by citizens of a particular country. Focusing on the UK as an example of the type of demand for international sharing, we note that UK citizens are active travellers on business and holidays to continental Europe and elsewhere, just as the UK is a popular destination for European travellers.

Table 2.2 Travel and tourism. UK Incoming and outgoing visits 1989

Destination or home country	*UK residents travelling abroad (000s visits)*		*European residents travelling to UK (000s visits)*	
		% *		% *
Spain	6 171	23	613	6
France	6 468	25	2 254	21
Greece	1 625	6	126	1
Irish Republic	2 010	8	1 302	12
West Germany	1 652	6	2 010	19
Italy	1 288	5	700	6
Netherlands	1 123	4	945	8
Portugal	998	4	93	1
Gibraltar/Malta/Cyprus	1 091	4	†	–
Yugoslavia	551	2	†	–
Belgium	775	3	589	5
Luxembourg	49	–	26	–
Austria	649	2	146	1
Switzerland	601	2	418	4
Norway/Sweden/Finland	332	1	923	9
Denmark	160	0.5	256	2
Other	319	1	16	1
TOTAL	**26 310**		**10 787**	

* May not add up to 100% because of rounding.   † Included in others.
Source: Overseas Travel and Tourism Business Monitor MQ6 HMSO.

Table 2.2 is a detailed analysis of travel and tourism both by UK residents travelling abroad and by Europeans travelling to the UK. As this figure shows, the scope for international ATM sharing is immense.

INTERNATIONAL ATM SHARING ACHIEVED TO DATE

The use of UK ATM cards in international ATMs was pioneered by the UK national ATM network LINK, with some LINK card issuers becoming members in 1987 of the PLUS network of 52 000 ATMs and 120 million card holders in the USA, Japan, Canada, New Zealand, the Caribbean and other countries.

In Europe, the first connections to shared ATM networks have been achieved through the agreement of Nexus Payment Systems International and the Spanish and Portuguese networks, SISTEMA 4B and SIBS, with a combined total of 5300 ATMs and 9 million card holders. This agreement has been followed by further ones with Banksys in Belgium, SIA in Italy and Yapi Kredit in Turkey, thereby bringing a further 8500 ATMs and 13.5 million card holders into the combined sharing scenario. It is likely that the LINK connections to PLUS and the Nexus bilateral connections will extend in the near future to other European countries and to electronic funds transfer at point of sale schemes within these countries.

It is important to bear in mind that the further potential for international ATM sharing arrangements between other European countries is considerable, even though the density of ATM installations and their frequency of usage varies considerably between countries. The trend in ATM installations in all European countries is towards growth, as illustrated in Table 2.3.

An additional impetus towards full international reciprocity of ATMs will come from the European Commission. The European Council for Payment Systems has highlighted this reciprocity as being of importance in the move towards a single European market. The Commission is likely to place banks

Table 2.3 Growth in number of ATM installations by country Jan. 1988–Jan. 1989

Country	Jan. 1988	Jan. 1989	% Increase 1988–1989
Austria	539	724	34
Belgium	833	985	18
Denmark	571	670	17
Finland	1 563	2 114	35
France	11 167	11 457	3
Germany	4 400	5 160	17
Greece	75	90	20
Ireland	293	371	27
Italy	3 500	4 227	21
Luxembourg	39	42	8
Netherlands	479	1 166	143
Norway	1 199	1 557	30
Portugal	377	586	55
Spain	7 092	8 916	26
Sweden	1 640	1 742	6
Switzerland	1 441	1 942	35
UK	12 389	14 116	14
TOTAL	**47 597**	**55 865**	**17**

Source: Battelle Institute.

and building societies under increasing pressure to open their networks to international card holders.

Participants in the LINK/PLUS connection are Abbey National PLC, AIB Bank, Britannia Building Society, Co-operative Bank PLC, Coventry Building Society, Girobank PLC, Nationwide Building Society, Western Trust Limited and Yorkshire Building Society.

There are currently 4.3 million card holders from financial institutions participating in the Nexus bilateral agreements, including AIB Bank, Britannia Building Society, Chelsea Building Society, Derbyshire Building Society, Dunfermline Building Society, Girobank PLC, Northern Rock Building Society, the Royal Bank of Scotland and the Yorkshire Building Society.

THE BENEFITS TO FINANCIAL INSTITUTIONS OF INTERNATIONAL ATM SHARING

International ATM sharing clearly offers many exciting possibilities to financial institutions. These advantages derive from the high level of consumer utility which international sharing offers. However, it is also useful to focus on the benefits which international ATM sharing can offer to those financial institutions which participate in it.

The basic point to make here is that international ATM sharing can help a financial institution add significant value to its plastic card services in terms of the benefit that customers derive from these services. International ATM sharing also provides institutions with many possibilities for obtaining high profile promotional coverage, e.g. through holiday competitions and general press coverage. For example, during the late 1908s one medium-sized UK building society obtained substantial national press coverage for a competition related to the launch of its PLUS connection. Estimates from one public relations company put the coverage at worth about £50 000 in advertising value. In this context, it is worth noting that personal finance journalists generally look favourably at international ATM sharing as a means of furnishing travellers with foreign currency abroad.

As a result of these factors, there is little doubt that a significant opportunity exists for financial institutions successfully to launch an international ATM facility, particularly one covering countries which have high tourism levels. International ATM sharing might reasonably be seen as an extension of national current account facilities. It can only be of growing relevance in an international climate where many people are enjoying increasingly international lifestyles.

It is very likely that an important key to the success of a new international ATM service will be the effectiveness of the methods that the institution in question uses to publicize it. There is a need to break down the current confusion between charge card, credit card and debit card access to ATMs. The fact that international ATM sharing operates with debit cards, and accesses a current or savings account rather than a credit or charge line must be emphasized and reiterated to card holders. Card holders will also naturally need to know which foreign institutions are participating in the ATM sharing arrangement and, more importantly, where their ATMs are located. The best solution to this requirement is for the home institution to issue a directory (or other list) of foreign ATM locations and branding.

Pricing and other membership criteria must also be considered. In general, international ATM sharing agreements with foreign banks will be subject to acquirer fees, which will either conform to an overall major international branding standard or will be specific to the particular agreement. For example, Eurocheque standards require issuer/acquirer transaction settlement at 1.3% of the amount withdrawn plus a fixed fee per transaction, and local call public telephone costs.

For the Nexus connections, pricing of ATM owner fees is based on eurocheque standards but open for negotiation between the participating bankers and networks.

As far as pricing to card holders is concerned, where this is not expressly covered in the international agreements themselves, this will naturally be at the discretion of the financial institution which issues the cards. Given the current high level of charges to customers of other travel facilities there is considerable scope for the card-issuer to charge commission for the international ATM transaction – thereby maintaining a good profit margin over costs – yet still to remain highly competitive as compared with the prices of other methods by which a traveller can be furnished with foreign currency abroad. Of course, as transaction volumes increase, international ATM sharing will become an important source of profit, with the service likely to become a dominant – if not the dominant – means of international cash provision.

In summary, the advantages for financial institutions of participating in an international ATM sharing arrangement are as follows.

1. The institution gains a low-cost international extension to

its distribution network to serve the needs of customers travelling abroad.

2. The likelihood of increased customer loyalty through high real (and perceived) added value.
3. A progressive image for promotional activities.
4. Low-cost, low-risk strategic positioning as part of activities related to the introduction of the single market in 1992.
5. The scope to charge customers a profitable commission that still undercuts other methods of providing foreign currency abroad.
6. Improved return on investment in ATMs from income generated by the millions of incoming travellers who use financial institutions' own ATMs.

GUIDELINES FOR WINNING CUSTOMERS WITH ATMS

1. Opt for an ATM system that operates in real-time. This not only greatly reduces losses due to fraud, but also provides the opportunity to extend a wider and more up-to-date range of services to customers.
2. Make the ATM central to new types of account, rather than operating the ATM as a peripheral benefit. Customers like using ATMs, and this fact should be exploited in branding and marketing strategies relating to new types of account.
3. Seek to minimize the downtime (i.e. inoperational time) of your institution's ATMs. Customers will want to rely on an ATM being available.
4. If you decide to participate in a shared ATM network, do more than pay lip-service to the concept of the shared network, but fully support your network's branding and marketing operations. The greater the extent to which people become familiar with conducting transactions across your network, the more popular your ATMs will be.
5. Exploit to the full the potential offered by interactive, colour and lobby ATMs for providing a wide range of customer services and for extending customer service into other, more profitable business areas. In particular, seek to exploit the

ATM's potential for allowing customers to arrange a personal service such as a loan, without the necessity of a potentially embarrassing conversation with a human teller.

CHAPTER THREE

Electronic Funds Transfer at Point of Sale (EFTPoS)

THE NATURE OF EFTPoS

EFTPoS is an electronic payment method which involves goods or services being paid for at the point of sale. The transaction may be initiated either by the EFTPoS card being 'swiped' through a card-reading device prior to the authorization of the transaction by means of a Personal Identification Number (PIN) being inputed into a hand-held pad by the customer, or else through the card swipe being followed by the customer signing a paper voucher.

METHODS OF ENACTING THE DEBIT

Although the fundamental principle of EFTPoS is the same however the transaction is initiated or actioned, there are four different ways in which the debit can be made. These are:

◆ real-time (i.e. instant) debit against a current or savings account;
◆ real-time debit against a credit account;
◆ debit after the usual clearing period (three days in the UK) against a current or savings account;
◆ debit after the usual clearing period against a credit account.

CHOOSING HOW TO ENACT THE DEBIT

The choice as to whether the debit should take place against a credit or current account is, assuming that the facilities are available, very much up to the customer. There are arguments in favour both of the debit taking place in real-time or after three days; the principal ones being that real-time debit allows customers to keep careful track of their expenditure, but forces them to forego the 'float' during the clearing period, whereas debit after the clearing period gives them the float but is less efficient in terms of allowing them to keep track of the state of their accounts. Many financial institutions have proved to be unwilling to commit themselves to one form of debit rather than to another; presumably because, although real-time debit appears to be the most 'perfect' form of EFTPoS, it involves the requirement that EFTPoS technology should operate in real-time at any time. Most institutions prefer to retain the option that even a real-time system should be able to operate in float mode on occasion.

BENEFITS OF EFTPoS TO CONSUMERS

The benefits of EFTPoS to consumers are not quite as self-evident as the benefits of ATMs, or of national or international ATM sharing. It appears likely that in due course EFTPoS will become a dominant payment method in all the countries where it is implemented – indeed, in the UK it is rapidly becoming this now – but any financial institution which wishes to participate in an EFTPoS scheme must accept that it has a two-fold educational task ahead of it to persuade both consumers and retailers of the benefits of the system.

Since it is reasonable to say that the overall pros and cons of EFTPoS are still in a state of flux, it is perhaps inadvisable to make any sweeping generalizations here regarding the ultimate likelihood of EFTPoS becoming widely accepted around Europe as a dominant payment method except to say that it appears that consumers are gradually becoming alive to the advantages of EFTPoS. Further evidence of this will be found in Chapter Seven, which looks at the state of play of electronic payment systems – including EFTPoS – around Europe. However, it would be foolish for any institution to ignore the perceived *disadvantages* of EFTPoS to themselves, retailers and consumers. Table 3.1 provides an overview of the advantages and disadvantages of EFTPoS to institutions, retailers and consumers. The reader will see that some of the disadvantages depend on uncertainty over consumer acceptability of EFTPoS, and that these detracting factors would erode as consumer acceptability of EFTPoS increases.

SHOULD AN INSTITUTION JOIN A SHARED EFTPoS NETWORK?

Another area of relative uncertainty for financial institutions seeking to become involved in EFTPoS is the extent to which they ought to become involved in shared EFTPoS schemes, or develop their own initiatives. On the face of it, the advantages of participating in shared schemes appear considerable. As with shared ATM networks, the advantages which participants in shared EFTPoS schemes would include:

◆ cost advantages through the sharing of terminals;
◆ the opportunity to participate in a shared branded EFTPoS network will probably reduce individual participants' marketing costs;
◆ the sharing of knowledge and expertise is likely to lead to higher levels of these throughout the network;
◆ a large shared EFTPoS network is likely to be more secure than numerous smaller networks (and security is of course a prime consideration of an EFTPoS network).

These advantages of shared network participation are incontestable. However, it is equally true that institutions themselves see EFTPoS as offering extensive opportunities for establishing a competitive advantage over rival institutions, and are consequently likely to remain in a state of relative uncertainty between recognizing the advantages of joining a shared net-

Table 3.1 Advantages and disadvantages of electronic funds transfer at point of sale

	Financial Institution	Retailer	Customer
Advantages	1. Enormous opportunities for generating commission revenue exist. 2. Widely implemented, EFTPoS would greatly reduce the mass of cheques which institutions must process every day.	1. Cash handling costs reduced. 2. Fewer dishonoured cheques. 3. Better central management control of payments in. 4. Lower bank transaction charges. 5. More productivity in the back office.	1. No need to carry cash, fewer security problems. 2. Transaction can be made quickly and conveniently. 3. Customer can monitor state of account on a transaction-by-transaction basis in some cases. 4. Possible increased status. 5. No need to write a cheque. 6. No need to carry a cheque book.
Disadvantages	1. Initial investment required is high. 2. No clear evidence is available that most customers want EFTPoS. 3. Many retailers are opposed to EFTPoS. 4. Single national EFTPoS do not often exist.	1. No clear evidence exists that allowing a customer to debit a current account is an incentive for customers to spend money that would not otherwise be spent. (With credit cards there *is* this incentive.) 2. Unauthorized transactions could cause loss of customer goodwill.	1. PIN or other authorization code must be memorized. 2. Card may be lost. 3. If system debits instantly customer loses three day grace period provided by cheques. 4. If cashier cannot get authorization customer may suffer embarrassment. 5. The customer may simply be indifferent to EFTPoS.

work, or forming their own EFTPoS network. No better example of this uncertainty is seen than in the somewhat unfortunate history of EftPoS UK.

THE STORY OF EftPoS UK

The foundations of EftPoS UK were laid in December 1986, when the Bank of England, and a number of major financial institutions belonging to the Association for Payment Clearing Services (APACS), launched a national EFTPoS strategy. From the outset, there was tension between EftPoS UK and some of its members who, while continuing to be EftPoS UK members, had also initiated plans to develop their own EFTPoS systems. During 1986 and 1989 two of the original members, Girobank and the Nationwide Anglia (now Nationwide) Building Society, pulled out of EftPoS UK, although, hedging their bets, both stated that they wanted to retain the options of rejoining EftPoS UK at a later date, presumably as and when EftPoS UK showed itself to be a viable system.

But this was not to be, although EftPoS UK's general manager, Brian Allison, had frequently made it clear that he would accept no compromises in the need to grow EftPoS UK into a nationwide EFTPoS system – the first such nationwide system in the world. The original idea was for EftPoS UK to start by deploying 2000 terminals in an Inaugural Service in Edinburgh, Leeds and Southampton, a service which began deployment in summer 1989. EftPoS UK subsequently announced that the Inaugural Service was proving a success, and that plans were afoot to develop it into a nationwide service. Then suddenly on 24 January 1990, EftPoS UK announced that it had abandoned its plans for a national EFTPoS service, which meant, in effect, that EftPoS UK was being scrapped. This move would have surprised those who had followed the apparently continually improving fortunes of EftPoS UK over the previous two years, but not those who had seen the great increase in individual banks' own EFTPoS initiatives.

The decision to cancel EftPoS UK was contained in a deliberately low-key press release issued by APACS, EftPoS UK's parent company.

Brian Allison subsequently said that he and his team at EftPoS UK were disappointed with the decision to terminate the service; a decision, Allison said, which had been taken for the simple reason that the individual EftPoS UK members' initiatives in such areas as debit cards and EFTPoS systems (branded cards such as Connect and Switch, in other words) had become so dominating that an individually-branded national EFTPoS service was no longer competitively viable.

Whether or not EftPoS UK has any role to play within APACS and national EFTPoS developments in future, there is no denying that the loss of EftPoS UK from the UK retail financial technology scene was a sad one. For more than two years Allison and his team had brought a welcome breeze of enterprise, optimism and enthusiasm into the retail electronic payments scenario.

However, in the end, EftPoS UK's members simply did not have the commitment to a national EFTPoS scheme that was required if the scheme was to work. And so, instead of the gradual development of such a scheme, the British shopper now has the choice of a variety of two competing national schemes (Connect and Switch) neither of which are compatible with each other.

CASE STUDY FOUR   EFTPoS IN THE UK TODAY

Chapter Seven looks at EFTPoS initiatives throughout Europe. Meanwhile, the remainder of this chapter focuses on the development of EFTPoS in what might reasonably be called a pioneering market for this electronic payment system – the UK.

The example of the UK is particularly pertinent here, as the UK occupies a special position in the European debit card debate. In the UK, following the introduction of debit cards linked to a current account, separate pricing for credit cards and debit cards has become widely established. The response to retailers once they realized that they would have to pay credit card commission rates on transactions on Barclays Bank's 'Connect' card was uniformly hostile and forced Barclays to step back from this charging policy. At the time, during what was a very heated public debate (with the media the setting for the debate, as is usually the case with this type of debate nowadays) an argument that retailers often used was that, unlike credit cards, debit cards did not inspire consumers to make transactions that they would otherwise not have made, because consumers know that credit cards allow them to defer payment. Whether this argument is sound or not – and obviously it is difficult to prove this particular matter either way – there is no doubt that UK retailers see debit cards as being related to cheques and cash payments, and credit card payments as belonging to a very different area of payments. However, this perception of a polarization between two types of method of payment is something which is unique to the UK. On Continental Europe the same resistance to charging for credit card and debit card transactions is not in evidence. As a result, the UK environment offers very interesting and exciting possibilities for EFTPoS to be clearly differentiated from credit card transactions.

Visa

The first major debit card schemes in the UK were issued under Visa branding in 1987. The first was Barclays Bank's 'Connect' card, which currently offers the following functions combined in one card:

◆ a debit card for payment anywhere that displays the Visa sign;
◆ a cheque guarantee card for up to £50 or £100;
◆ a cash dispenser card.

The choice of Visa branding was intended to ensure the immediate wide availability of cards through the Visa 'honour all cards' rule whereby merchants who are Visa members are obliged to accept the card. The second motive was to maintain credit card commission structures whereby the retailer accepting a Visa branded debit card was being required to pay, say, between 1–5% of the transaction amount to the merchant acquirer in the same way as when accepting a credit card. In hindsight this was a somewhat optimistic expectation on the part of Barclays, particularly bearing in mind that a large retailer may pay only a few pence to the merchant acquirer for clearing a cheque, and Barclays Connect was, after all, a cheque replacement product. In the event, retailer reactions to Barclays Connect were immediate, hostile and effective; forcing Barclays to climb down and introduce cheque clearing equivalent fees for the larger retailers.

The Lloyds Bank Payment Card, the combined debit card, cheque guarantee and cashpoint card offered by Lloyds is also based on the Visa branding in order for the customer to identify outlets where it can be used.

There are currently more than 2.6 million Barclays Connect cards and 2 million Lloyds Payment Visa cards in circulation. Lloyds claim the number of cards to be increasing at 150 000 per month. These 4.6 million cards can be used at 380 000 retail outlets bearing the Visa sign. TSB has launched its '3 in 1 Bankcard', which incorporates a Visa debit facility. Only 9000 retailers offering a total of 12 000 terminals can capture Visa debit card transactions electronically. The Visa UK market-place has predominantly consisted to date of small- to medium-sized retailers.

Retailers are charged on a per transaction rate of 6–15p depending on size and negotiating strength. Debits are made directly to the card-holder's current account on a three day cycle to mirror cheque clearing. The cards can operate in EFTPoS terminals such as Processes Data Quickly (PDQ), Accept and Cardpoint, or can be used in paper voucher systems.

It is reasonable to say that Visa debit cards have achieved their wide acceptability at the price of some confusion among both consumers and retailers. Consumers are faced with a recognized credit card brand that has a markedly different function from credit cards. Similarly, retailers have until recently had no easy means of identifying whether a card is a debit card with transaction charges, or a credit card with percentage commissions. Other retailers have turned to promoting 'Switch' cards which have not suffered from such ambiguity.

The resulting pressure on Visa has led to Visa granting important concessions. The 'honour all cards' rule has been relaxed; Visa has created the 'Electron' debit card and has established a (still very restricted) class of 'E' retailers who can choose to accept the Electron card without being obliged to accept Visa credit cards. This means that the Visa 'Classic' and 'Premier' cards remain primarily credit card brands. An Electron logo for cards and appropriate shop signage has been developed.

Although Visa's launch of an EFTPoS service was a little shakey (as pioneering work often is), Visa is currently making great efforts to position its EFTPoS initiatives in line with the requirements of institutions, retailers and consumers. In June 1991, at a forum for senior executives of financial institutions, Patrick Bowden, general manager of marketing and strategy for Visa International's Europe, Middle East and African region, outlined Visa's conceptual approach to debit cards. The following is a slightly amplified version of his comments. Although Bowden was relating his thoughts to the EFTPoS initiatives of Visa, they are equally relevant if applied to EFTPoS as a whole.

> When we planned the Visa debit card product for the UK, our first step was to set up a Debit Card Working Group, which then consulted with all UK Visa members (and many non-members) and which also sought the views of members and retail bodies such as the Retail Consortium [an influential UK retailers' association].
>
> We listened to what these people had to say, and we made their comments and reflections part of our overall understanding of the way in which the changes are taking place within the UK payment environment. In particular, we noted that while credit cards are increasingly being used for convenience, the profitability of credit cards is declining. We saw quite clearly that there was considerable

scope for us to win business by deploying new payment methods to retailers and consumers who were already familiar with the Visa name. In doing this we would also be meeting a real need, as institutions and retailers were anxious to address the question of costs of processing and handling cheques, not to say the security problems which are inevitably attached to what is increasingly an old-fashioned means to pay for goods at the point of sale.

We were – and remain – particularly interested in meeting the needs of the building societies. We are well aware that the needs of the societies from an EFTPoS organization are not the same as those of the clearing banks. Like the clearers, building societies must also attract and retain customers, but in many ways the societies have shown themselves to be more interested in building relationships with customers and obtaining retail deposits at the lowest possible price to support the societies' traditional mortgage business. With consumer requirements evolving and competition fierce, the societies indicated to us that they only attracted about 10% of the 'new to banking' markets. The societies also said that they needed a debit card which offered the best customer proposition, and in particular wide acceptances for purchases and cash withdrawal, so as to balance the relatively small size of societies' branch networks compared to the major banks, while maintaining control over fraud and the risks of bad debts.

At Visa we have concluded that a successful debit card system must meet certain key requirements, which can be summarized as follows.

Firstly, the system must have wide acceptability among retailers. This is by far the most critical success factor. **Ultimately, acceptability drives usage**. The debit card is primarily a cheque substitute so it has to have the utility of a cheque, and this means that consumers must have ample opportunities to use it.

Secondly, the system must offer consumers additional levels of functionality. In other words, it must do something for them that existing payment systems are not doing. Customers are already relaxed about using cash and cheques; for debit cards to become popular they have to offer added value. In other words, the consumer must see the debit card and the system with which it is associated as providing a utility which is clearly beyond the limitations of the cheque book and the cheque guarantee card.

Thirdly, consumers must have confidence in the system. In practice, consumer confidence is closely allied to the acceptability of the system among retailers.

Fourthly, the system must have a proven infrastructure. To put it bluntly, the system has to work first time, every time! Furthermore, financial institutions do not have bottomless systems development pockets. Where a satisfactory infrastructure is already in place, there is every reason for the financial institution to use it.

Fifthly, there must be cost and revenue benefits for participants. What this means in practice is that potential card issuers will want to contain the costs of their money transmission services in both joining fees and usage. Participating institutions will also seek opportunities for revenue generation.

Finally, the system operator will need to show that it can provide back-up support. Participating institutions, particularly those new to money transmission, will want the comfort of knowing that a professional support team will be available, particularly during the implementation stage.

Switch

The Switch debit card scheme and delivery system was started by the Midland and NatWest banks and the Royal Bank of Scotland in April 1988. Since the launch of the system the Bank of Scotland, Barclays Bank, the Clydesdale/Northern Bank, the Halifax Building Society, the Yorkshire Bank, have joined as full members and card issuers. Smaller institutions, or institutions which do not require to be fully represented on Switch committees, often enter the system via 'Stasis', which is a Midland Bank-supported system for alternative entry to Switch.

Switch has been a considerable success, with about 12 million cards already issued and more than 150 000 Switch terminals across the country. This high level of terminal roll-out reflects the wide penetration of Switch among consumers and its acceptability among retailers. Indeed, by the summer of 1991 it was announced that Switch turnover had reached £4 billion per annum on 1.5 billion transactions, and that all the UK's 'Top 200' High Street retailers now accepted Switch.

The participants have certainly rolled out Switch with impressive speed. For example, at the start of 1990 there were only two Shell petrol stations in the UK with Switch facilities. By the end of 1991 most Shell petrol stations in Britain were equipped to take Switch. On average, more than 4000 terminals are being opened every month. Even Marks and Spencer, which is generally regarded as being averse to other organizations' plastic cards, is experimenting with Switch. The recent development of a new low-cost free standing/hand held terminal will also enable Switch to be extended to medium and small retailers.

As an example of the kind of investment in infrastructure that Switch participation requires, consider the case of the Midland bank, which has estimated that the Switch programme has cost it in the vicinity of £30 million. However, in return for this, Midland is already anticipating an overall reduction of up to 50% in its costs of processing paper-based payments. This adds up to hundreds of millions of pounds each year.

Each full Switch member is responsible for its own card programme and for acquiring transactions. A member also has the option to acquire merchants on behalf of the scheme. Switch members compete with each other for these merchant relationships. The merchant tariffing and clearing cycle are similar to those of Visa debit cards. Switch is developing as an open system and appears willing to accept new members as card issuers, including smaller financial institutions.

The success of Switch in the UK in the short period since its formation contrasts sharply – and favourably – with EftPoS UK. Even to an impartial observer, it is fair to conclude that Switch has become an important standard for EFTPoS in the UK. Pointers indicating this success are as follows.

1. UK consumers appear to be coming to realize the benefits of Switch. Unquestionably there is still an educational task ahead in order to persuade the maximum number of consumers to change from a cheque-based to an EFTPoS-based payment mentality, but Switch has certainly gained considerable headway with consumers.
2. The Switch card base is considerably larger than the *combined* total of the Lloyds and Barclays Visa debit card base.
3. Switch is indisputably a debit card. Unlike Visa, it has no ambiguity attached to it. The clarity of the Switch concept has undoubtedly proved attractive to major retailers.
4. Switch has gained wholehearted support from eight major financial institutions, and from many smaller ones.
5. There has been a high initial take-up of Switch by the volume-orientated national retail chains (grocery and petrol).
6. Switch has been able to show itself to be a practical solution; building on retailers' existing technology by supporting their terminals.
7. The system has what is perceived to be a fair charging structure for retailers based on per transaction charges.
8. The 'semi-off-line' technology favoured by Switch – which uses signature verification and either a three-day 'float' or real-time debit.

The Application by Barclays Bank and Lloyd's Bank to join Switch

As a rider to the above information readers should note that in October 1989 Barclays Bank and Lloyds Bank both agreed to join Switch solely as merchant acquirers and not as card issuers. Initially both banks had their applications turned down. Subsequently Barclays and Lloyds complained to the Office of Fair Trading (OFT) that the refusal on the part of Switch to admit them amounted to a restrictive practice.

The dispute centred around the lucrative £500 million UK market for processing plastic card acquisitions on behalf of retailers. This is a service known as merchant acquisition. Lloyds and Barclays saw an important opportunity for acquiring Switch transactions in addition to the card schemes that they already supported.

However, Switch had rules which prevented banks from becoming acquirers unless they issued Switch branded cards and that their Switch card is their 'main debit card'. This conflicted with Barclays' Connect card and the Lloyds Bank payment card (both Visa cards). These rules were the subject of the OFT investigation. Although the OFT did not take any legal action against Switch, it did ask Switch to remove the rule specifying that only banks with Switch as their main debit card could become acquirers. The OFT said that this rule was 'anti-competitive'.

The Lloyds Bank application has now lapsed, and at present it appears that Lloyds is perfectly happy with its own Visa payment card and has no further interest in joining Switch. However, Barclays became a full Switch member in August 1990, at which time it outlined plans to start acting as a Switch acquirer, and to issue its own Switch card, 'during the second half of 1991'. Barclays has not yet indicated what branding will be attached to its Switch card.

THE SAINSBURY'S AND TESCO EXPERIENCE OF EFTPoS

The two UK supermarket chains Sainsbury's and Tesco have played a major role in the rapid expansion of EFTPoS in the UK. Taken together, Sainsbury's and Tesco account for almost 30% of all retail grocery sales in the UK.

Retail grocery is obviously an area where the utility of EFTPoS is likely to be at a premium. The entire development of retail food marketing, worldwide, during the past thirty years has focused on customer self-service and the rapid passage of customers through the checkouts. Inevitably, large food stores must handle very high volumes of individual transactions every day. Customers, too, may be expected to see the advantages in being able to pay for transactions rapidly and without needing to write a cheque or rely on cash.

In the case of Sainsbury's, the group's interest in EFTPoS dates back to November 1987, when it began experimental trials of EFTPoS in some stores in conjunction with Girobank. The group was encouraged by these trials, and during 1989 Sainsbury's mounted a major drive to convert its customers to using Switch debit cards to pay for purchasers.

As of July 1991 Sainsbury's accepted all UK EFTPoS cards; that is, Switch-branded cards, Barclays Connect, the Lloyds Visa payment card and the TSB debit card. Remarkably enough, 10%, by total sum, of all check out payments at Sainsbury's now come via EFTPoS. EFTPoS is operated at all Sainsbury's stores that feature electronic scanning which is the vast majority of the stores.

Another interesting development at Sainsbury's, and other major UK retailers has been the start of trials of the 'Cashback' service. This service – which is surely destined to become popular wherever EFTPoS is popular, although perhaps progressing more slowly than the parent service – is based on the sound principle that allowing retail customers to withdraw cash from a till that is likely to be cash-rich not only represents a useful service for the customer, but also helps to reduce the retailer's security problems inherent in holding large sums of cash.

Sainsbury's current facility allows customers with Switch to draw up to £50 in cash as part of the transaction. Sainsbury's estimates that about 10% of its customers who use EFTPoS will eventually also use Cashback.

Sainsbury's has found that, despite the group's initial concern about this, customers do not appear to mind losing the 'three day' float which they would gain on cheque payments. Although EFTPoS at Sainsbury's nowadays involves overnight debits, the group does not believe that this has caused would-be EFTPoS users to refrain from taking advantage of this service.

Tesco, too, has been actively interested in EFTPoS since ideas for the service were first discussed. In October 1989 Tesco conducted EFTPoS trials at its Hatfield and Abingdon stores. The trials confirmed Tesco's belief that debit cards would take business from all other payment methods with the level of debit card business having a likely potential to run at about 15%. There was a reduction in credit card takings during the trials.

Tesco now takes all kinds of debit cards (including Switch, Connect and Visa debit cards) at all of its UK stores. In addition, Tesco runs store-based petrol stations which take Switch. Tesco intends all its stores to accept EFTPoS by 1993.

SMALLER RETAILERS AND EFTPoS

Finally, it is useful to consider the attitude which small retailers are likely to hold towards EFTPoS. For this purpose a small retailer might be considered as one with four checkouts or cash registers, or fewer. Garage forecourts and off-licences would be excluded from this definition, since here customer pressures has already made EFTPoS an established technique.

In April 1990, at the UK Retail EFTPoS conference, David Mendus, the chairman of Londis Computer Services – the computing services group of the independent retail grocery chain Londis – presented his views summarizing the situation for the small retailer. Mendus said that, in general, the level of interest in the particular EFTPoS-related needs which smaller retailers had was generally very low among EFTPoS operators. He also said that the smaller retailer probably sees EFTPoS as a complication, an expense and a way for the major multiples to tighten the screw further on the smaller retailers' profitability. The typical small retailer, Mendus said, 'is tending to hope that EFTPoS will go away and that he can continue to take cash and just a few cheques; the familiar payment methods'. He went on to say that in order to become attractive to the smaller retailer, EFTPoS had to be able to demonstrate an improvement in terms either of:

◆ costs;
◆ staff time;
◆ management time;
◆ business opportunity.

Mendus expanded on some possible technical solutions for the small retailer to be able to implement EFTPoS. He suggested that costs would inevitably be a major problem, suggested since the high capital costs of EFTPoS terminals would be likely to make EFTPoS unviable for smaller retailers from the outset. He did point out, however, that some EFTPoS operators had shown some interest in bringing out a lower-priced terminal which would give them the opportunity to address the smaller retailer market.

Interestingly, Mendus also acknowledged that smaller retailers recognize that they cannot afford to ignore EFTPoS completely, as it appears that banks are moving toward a situation where they will replace cheque processing by EFTPoS wherever possible. He stated that even if EFTPoS is unlikely to be cheaper to process than cheques, it is likely that cheques will, over the next few years, become more expensive to process than EFTPoS. This does indeed seem a likely scenario, and would play a part in which may soon turn out to be the inexorable rise of EFTPoS at the expense of cheques.

GUIDELINES FOR WINNING CUSTOMERS WITH EFTPoS

1. Arrive at a realistic assessment of whether your customers really want EFTPoS, and if they do, what kind of EFTPoS scheme they prefer. Consider the possibility of researching the attitude of your market in detail.
2. Accept that participation in a shared EFTPoS scheme will almost certainly be to your advantage.
3. Ensure that your EFTPoS scheme offers customers the

widest range of options in terms of how they can use the scheme. Customers should be allowed to choose whether to debit their transactions against a debit or credit account and whether to use a system involving a voucher which they sign at the point of sale, or else a purely electronic system.

4. Consider the advantages, in terms of marketing impact and convenience, of combining an ATM card with an EFTPoS card.

CHAPTER FOUR

Telephone banking

THE NATURE OF TELEPHONE BANKING

Telephone banking is a means for a financial institution to provide a more or less automated banking service to customers via the customer's own telephone. Since it makes use of electronics (in the form of communications equipment) it is a form of electronic payment system, with customers able to give banks a range of instructions, including payment instructions, over the telephone.

A BACKGROUND TO TELEPHONE BANKING

As the professional and leisure lives of banks' customers have ranged over wider geographical areas, the central role of the local banking branch in the delivery of banking services has become increasingly outdated. We have already seen how customers have turned to automated teller machines and EFTPoS to conduct transactions and to make payments by remote means. Many customers have also come to rely heavily on manual telephone and postal liaison with their banks in order to arrange payment facilities and obtain account information. Market research strongly supports the view that the demand for remote delivery will continue to increase. Figure 4.1 demonstrates the appeal of branchless banking to customers.

Figure 4.1 Appeal of branchless banking market research results

One in five people had not visited their branch in the last month

One in ten people had not visited their branch in the last six months

Over half (51%) said they would rather visit their bank as little as possible

Over a third (37%) used cash dispensers rather than withdrawing money over the counter inside their bank

On the last visit to their branch, one in three people had left without speaking to any bank staff

Nearly half (48%) had never met their bank manager. Of those who had, over a third (36%) said the meeting was over a year ago

Almost 40% (39%) complain that there are too many queues at banks

Almost 40% (38%) find it inconvenient to visit the bank because of short opening hours

Over a quarter (27%) wished they could do more business with banks by telephone

Source: First Direct (Battelle, August 1990).

It should, therefore, be no surprise that an important feature of the retail banking scene in the 1990s is a greatly increased demand among customers for direct bank-to-customer banking. Financial institutions are responding vigorously to this demand and are competing with each other to provide effective facilities for the remote delivery of banking services. The surge in competition over the provision of these services shows every sign of rivalling the initially US-wide and then Europe-wide competition over ATMs which took place in the 1970s and the 1980s.

OPTIONS FOR REMOTE BANKING SERVICE DELIVERY

The two principal options for the delivery of remote banking services are:

- services based around a personal computer (PC) located in the customer's home;
- services based around the customer's home telephone.

THE ADVANTAGES OF TELEPHONE BANKING

It is difficult not to conclude that the telephone-based option is likely to offer a much greater utility than the PC-based option. Telephone services are usually available 24 hours a day and can include automated systems, answerphones and person-to-person calls. In practical trials they have proved to be much more successful than PC-based home banking, which not only suffers from higher start-up costs but also requires the customer to have specialized equipment, which is also likely to be expensive either for the institution, the customer, or both.

Telephone-based contact also offer the great advantage that almost everybody is familiar with using the telephone as a communications tool, whereas very few people are adept at communicating via a computer. Telephone banking allows a financial institution to benefit from a low-cost extension to its distribution network, while the customer benefits from being able to conduct banking business wherever and whenever it is convenient.

A very full range of banking services can be offered by the telephone, thereby reducing the customer's need to visit a branch during opening hours. Only cash withdrawals and account deposits cannot be handled satisfactorily by telephone.

TECHNOLOGICAL OPTIONS FOR TELEPHONE BANKING

There are three major technology options in telephone banking, all of which had made substantial progress over the last few years towards becoming proven cost-effective technological solutions. In all instances, the computer responds to the caller in a clear speaking voice, which is created not by crude simulation but by digitizing a real voice speaking the range of expressions that are required for communication.

1. *Tone telephones/voice response*: an increasing number of modern push button telephones send an audible multi-frequency tone down a telephone line which can be interpreted electronically by a receiving computer. The customer input is therefore made by means of the tones. The system's response, however, is made by voice. In instances where a customer does not have a touch tone telephone then a special tone pad can be supplied which is held onto a standard telephone to create the necessary tones. The customer can communicate with the central computer by pushing the normal numbered buttons of the telephone or the tone pad according to easily comprehensible instructions.

2. *Pre-programmed telephones*: it is possible to provide telephones with keys which will select the banking transaction that is required by the customer. These telephones are easy to understand but require special equipment to be installed at the customer's home, which somewhat detracts from the advantage of simplicity and facility which telephone banking otherwise possesses.

3. *Voice recognition*: some telephone banking systems are able to recognize the spoken instructions of customers within a pre-programmed range of words, and respond accordingly. These systems are likely to be increasingly important in automated delivery as the technology develops. However, it is fair to say that, at least to date, failure rates of the technology are perhaps too high for financial institutions to have full confidence in the service without a multi-frequency tone fall-back. Indeed, in the US, manufacturers of voice recognition technology believe that it will always be most effectively used in conjunction with a multi-frequency tone capability.

LESSONS DRAWN FROM THE US EXPERIENCE

Perhaps the best evidence of the relative strengths of telephone banking, the manual and automated approaches to telephone banking comes from the US, where telephone banking is well established. Significantly, Bank of America, the major supplier of person-to-person telephone services, has converted to automated technology for the processing of routine transactions and now maintains the person-to-person service only for more advanced transactions. This gives the customer efficiency in routine banking and the option of calling for assistance from a human operator when necessary.

CONCLUSION

Practical industry experience strongly suggests that the best entry method into telephone banking is through a voice-response automated system. The best long-term solution is likely to be a combination of automated and human operation. This mirrors the way in which customers currently use ATMs for routine transactions, but deal with a specialist human operator for more involved banking business.

CASE STUDY FIVE   TELEPHONE BANKING IN THE UK

In the UK, the telephone banking systems which lead the market are based around tone telephone/voice-response technology. This technology has proved very popular with customers and gives a secure and proven level of service which allows a financial institution to maximize its return on investment. The costs of automated telephone banking services are a fraction of those associated with a fully-staffed service. Quality can be maintained at the highest levels.

One of the most highly publicized moves into telephone banking has been the First Direct service. Launched in 1989, First Direct is a wholly-owned (but independently operating) subsidiary of the Midland Bank, offering a full banking service through person-to-person telephone calls. By the beginning of

1991 First Direct had exceeded its target of 100 000 customers. The performance of the service to date has been successful, but for routine the person-to-person telephone banking approach does not appear to have many real advantages over an efficient automated delivery system. However, First Direct claims that its research indicates that given a choice of home banking methods, 76% of customers would prefer to speak to a real person than to a computer.

In the UK, the growth of automated telephone banking has been accelerated by a strong demand from financial institutions' customers. It is very unusual in banking for a service which has received so little media coverage to have achieved such impressive sales figures. During 1990 the milestone of one million UK telephone banking customers was reached for the retail banking sector as a whole.

However, the overall potential for telephone banking is much greater, with thousands of new customers being introduced to the service each week. Research by the UK-based research organization CMG and by other reputable industry sources indicates that between 15 and 20% of current account holders can be expected in due course to subscribe to telephone banking services. Suppliers expect, that over the next 5–10 years, the number of users will increase rapidly to the near saturation levels achieved by ATMs.

There are currently more than ten major financial institutions in the UK with a significant presence in the telephone banking arena. One of the most successful has been the TSB Bank and its SpeedLink service which has more than 25 000 customers. Nationwide Building Society's FlexAccount has over 100 000 customers for its Home Banking Service. Both these services are based on tone telephone voice response technology.

Suppliers of voice recognition services include Clydesdale Bank, Girobank and National Westminster Bank. Practical experience here shows that this type of service, while more expensive and subject to error/rejection problems, is also proving popular with customers.

Table 4.1 gives an overview of the UK telephone banking arena as of July 1991.

Table 4.1 The UK telephone banking arena

Institution	Name of service	Tone pad and voice response (T) or voice recognition (V)	Charge for tone pad/service	Charge per call
Alliance & Leicester Building Society	Cashplus Phone banking	T	£6.00	Full rate*
Clydesdale Bank PLC	Telebank Telephone service	T + V	£12.00	Full rate
Girobank PLC	Dialog Telephone Banking system	V	–	Full rate*
Halifax Building Society	Maxim Home banking	T + V	£6.00	Full rate*
Nationwide Building Society	FlexAccount Home banking service	T	£10 returnable deposit	Full rate*
National & Provincial Building Society	Max	T + V	£5 returnable deposit	Full rate*
Northern Rock Building Society	Home banking service	T	£7.99 or £2.50 charge quarterly	Full rate*
National Westminster Bank	Actionline Banking by telephone	T + V	Free tone pad. First 6 months service free, then £2.50 per quarter	Full rate
Royal Bank of Scotland	Phoneline	V	–	Local rate
TSB	Speedlink Banking by telephone	T	£6 + £2.50 per quarter (+ £5 per quarter if fax service is added)	Full rate*

* Assumption of full rate is made as no mention is made of cheaper calls.

THE RANGE OF SERVICES WHICH A FINANCIAL INSTITUTION CAN SUPPLY VIA A TELEPHONE

Experience suggests that institutions can provide a very broad range of banking services via the telephone, ranging from responses to simple enquiries regarding account balances on current, savings or mortgage accounts, through to complex loan applications.

In the UK, for example, the successful automated systems in the market-place are limited to straightforward and relatively simple transactions such as balance enquiries, bill payments, transfers between accounts, cheque book ordering, statement requests and information regarding interest rates. The provision of services in this range has proved to be the most successful with customers and the easiest for them to understand. Furthermore, these services do not involve the customers in lengthy telephone calls, which, considering that most customers must pay the full rate for phone calls, is just as well.

Table 4.2 shows a typical breakdown of transactions made by UK customers of telephone banking services.

Table 4.2 Typical telephone banking transaction breakdown

	% of total transactions
Balance enquiry	60
Account enquiry	20
Bill payments	10
Transfers between accounts	5
Other	5

Source: Industry Sources.

HOW A FINANCIAL INSTITUTION SHOULD PRICE A TELEPHONE BANKING SERVICE

In general, financial institutions which have entered the telephone banking market have found that customers are prepared to pay for the opportunity to use the service, although payment is in practice fairly nominal and in some cases relates merely to a kind of deposit for leasing the tone pad. The main business activity of providing the telephone banking service is funded out of the bank's overall operations budget, as is the institution's branch network. Institutions do not seek to obtain revenue from telephone calls made to the system (in contrast with many commercial organizations which advertise telephone lines where they receive a percentage of call charges from the telecommunications service provider). Indeed, some institutions subsidize telephone calls by providing a 'freephone' service, or by charging long-distance calls at a local rate. None the less, this tends to be the exception rather than the rule.

Note that there are three principal ways in which institutions derive revenue from customers for the opportunity to use a telephone banking service. These are as follows:

1. *Subscriptions*: it is not unusual for a regular charge to be levied for access to a telephone banking service. An institution will typically charge a certain quarterly fee (normally fairly nominal) for access to the basic telephone banking service and a higher quarterly fee for additional services, such as for a regular statement sent by fax.
2. *Start-up fee*: this typically involves charging the customer a small initial charge (perhaps in the region of £10) to establish them on the service.
3. *Returnable deposit*: some institutions request a returnable deposit from customers during the time that they are using the telephone banking service. The usual justification for the charge is that it is a deposit for the tone pad which will be supplied by the institution. For example, the Nationwide Building Society charges its telephone banking customers

£10 as a deposit. It should be noted that with more than
100 000 telephone banking customers this provides a substantial float for the Nationwide of over £1 million.

THE BUSINESS CASE FOR IMPLEMENTING A TELEPHONE BANKING SERVICE

The business case for telephone banking centres on the following considerations.

1. **The existing customer base**
   Depending on product positioning and the overall business
   and sales strategy, there is the short-to-medium likelihood
   of converting about 15–20% of the customer base on suitable
   accounts into users of the telephone banking service.
2. **The new customer base**
   In addition, if the telephone banking service is marketed
   effectively, it could be a key attraction for new primary
   account relationships; including new accounts switching
   from competitors and, even more critically, new entrants to
   the market.
3. **Revenue**
   Based on the analysis above.
4. **Cost savings**
   The automation of routine banking transactions leads to
   substantial cost savings for any financial institution over
   counter-based transactions (provided that counter transactions have been properly costed). In order to maximize
   these benefits it is important to automate those transactions
   which are typically conducted at the counter. A quick analysis of branch counter activity should easily identify where
   the major savings are likely to come. Savings of between
   25p and £1 per transaction would be realistic.

THE EXPECTED PRODUCT LIFE CYCLE

There are strong parallels between the development of telephone banking and that of ATMs. The rate at which telephone banking progresses will vary from country to country, although the overall progress of the service is likely to be rapid.

In the UK, the market for telephone banking services has now moved past the inception stage of high risk and uncertain return on technology and has entered a period of rapid growth. It is anticipated that during the next few years the telephone delivery of banking services will become an expected part of the normal customer banking relationship.

It is consequently very important that any financial institution wishing to create competitive advantage out of this new delivery system should act quickly. In the UK the window of opportunity for gaining customers from the service is only likely to last until about 1993. The option to 'do nothing' is unlikely to be a viable strategy for any financial institution. Should the take-up continue to grow as expected, financial institutions not offering the service in a few years' time are likely to be at a serious disadvantage.

THE OPTIONS FOR TELEPHONE CONNECTION

Financial institutions can decide on the type of telephone connection which they offer to their customers. The major options would be as follows:

1. a freephone service (in the UK, this is based on an 0800 number);
2. a local charge structure (in the UK, based on an 0345 number);
3. a normal trunk dialling rate attracting full charges.

Options one and two both involve the financial institution subsidizing, or partly subsidizing, the cost of the calls.

In the market-place, financial institutions have successfully adopted both local and full rate charging structures, although to date in the UK only the Royal Bank of Scotland has subsidized calls by adopting a local rate call system.

SELLING THE TELEPHONE BANKING SERVICE

The concept of banking by telephone is readily understood by customers. It is, however, necessary for an institution to provide customers with a telephone-based demonstration service which offers proof and reassurance that an automated service works in practice and is simple to use. Generally speaking, take-up is very strong by customers who witness a demonstration of the service, either in-branch or by calling special demonstration numbers set up by the financial institution. Trying to sell a telephone banking service without a demonstration of some kind is unlikely to result in a loyal regular user of the system.

Experience has shown that the service is likely to be most successful on current account type products and for multiple account holdings where the customer is looking to optimize the return by transferring to and from higher interest accounts.

SUMMARY OF BENEFITS OF TELEPHONE BANKING TO CUSTOMERS

The over-riding benefit to customers of a telephone banking service is the sheer convenience which the service will offer. Telephone banking has clear advantages over branch-based delivery, banking by post and even service via ATMs. The convenience benefits, which are more or less self-evident, relate to the following matters.

1. **Location**
   The customer can conduct his or her banking business from the home, office, car or anywhere else where a convenient telephone can be found, whether the customer is at home or abroad.
2. **Speed of transaction**
   Telephone calls are quickly and efficiently processed with

no need to make a special trip to the bank or building society branch, and with no need to queue to be served.

3. **Availability**

   The service can be made available 24 hours a day, 365 days a year, giving customers complete control regarding when they monitor their accounts. Telephone banking is also likely to prove particularly attractive to account holders who live in rural areas, or who otherwise – for reasons such as of ill health or pressure of work – do not find it easy to visit a branch of their financial institution.

Against these advantages of the service must be set the only apparent drawback; that the customer may have to pay a small fee for using the service and/or a deposit for holding the tone pad, and also will probably have to pay some telephone charges. However, as we have seen, the fees or deposits are in practice quite small. As for the telephone calls, even if they are not completely or partly subsidized by the institution, the duration of calls is likely to be no more than a minute or so at most. Besides, visiting a branch or ATM will usually also involve a cost – whether a fare or the cost of petrol. In practice, customers do not appear to consider that the charges associated with telephone banking represent a major disincentive to subscribing to, and using, the service.

SUMMARY OF BENEFITS OF TELEPHONE BANKING TO FINANCIAL INSTITUTIONS

Telephone banking is an attractive option from the point of view of the financial institution. The reasons for this are as follows.

1. Telephone banking provides the opportunity for a significant extension of the financial institution's distribution network at low cost, offering a round-the-clock services to customers and the possibility of extending a service to customers who live in geographically remote areas.
2. The service has, to date, proved popular with customers

and can be expected to make a significant contribution to building customer loyalty and attracting new primary account relationships.

3. Transactions processed by automated systems always cost an institution less to process than counter-based transactions. In this respect it is particularly important to note that over time the existence of telephone-based customer support is likely to reduce a financial institution's requirement to take on additional staff to handle increasing transaction volumes.

4. The introduction of telephone banking should provide a strong promotional opportunity for the financial institution and should also contribute to its progressive image.

GUIDELINES FOR WINNING CUSTOMERS WITH TELEPHONE BANKING

1. Make sure that the technology you are deploying is foolproof and easy to understand. At present, the use of a tone telephone/voice response system is probably more reliable than voice-recognition technology.

2. As with ATMs, an important way to emphasize to customers the added value provided by the telephone banking facility is to launch new types of accounts in which the telephone banking service features prominently rather than simply to add on the service as an 'appendix' to an existing account.

3. As with ATMs, minimizing the downtime of the telephone banking service is very important if customer confidence is to be established and maintained.

4. It is a reasonable supposition that customers will like your telephone banking service all the more, the cheaper it is for them to use.

CHAPTER FIVE

Smart cards

INTRODUCTION

Unlike the three principal types of electronic payment systems examined so far in this book, smart cards still have to make their mark within the retail financial sector, and at present must be regarded as an experimental form of electronic payment system in most countries. However, there is every indication that they are likely to play an increasing role in the retail financial sector as the 1990s proceed, and it is therefore useful to provide a discussion of smart cards here.

Readers should note that although in most European countries (including the UK) smart cards are still in the inception phase, the technology is far more developed in France, where smart cards might reasonably be said to be no longer in the inception phase, but to have moved to the growth phase.

THE NATURE OF SMART CARDS

Superficially, a smart card looks very much like any other plastic card, such as a credit card or a bank card. A smart card is almost invariably the same shape as a conventional plastic card. It may even be embossed and have a magnetic stripe on the back. However, it is there that the resemblance ends, as the smart card is not just another bank card but in essence, a miniature computer. Embedded in the card is a microcomputer chip giving it a processing power and a memory capacity far beyond that of today's magnetic strip cards. Indeed, a typical smart card of the 1990s has as much computing power as the personal computers of the early 1980s.

The advantage which smart cards offer to financial institutions and their customers is that being, in effect, tiny computers, they can be programmed to perform any task within their processing power and memory capacity. This means that instead of being essentially passive electronic tokens – which is basically what standard plastic cards are – smart cards can have a very wide range of functions; a range of functions, moreover, which can only increase as smart card technology develops.

POSSIBILITIES FOR IMPLEMENTING SMART CARDS WITHIN THE RETAIL FINANCIAL SECTOR

In terms of potential applications of smart cards within the retail financial services sector, there appear to be four major types of possible applications.

1. **The smart card as an information library**
   The card can be used as a convenient, portable and secure means of storing a wide range of information.
2. **The smart card as an identification tool**
   The smart card can provide an exceptionally secure means of identifying the user. There are two reasons for this. Firstly, the smart card can hold far more information about a particular user than a standard plastic card. Secondly, it is impossible to copy a smart card, since even if a duplicate card can be made the chip will need to be programmed with exactly the same information and instructions that the original card contained.
3. **The smart card as multi-function card**
   The processing and information storage power of smart cards means that a single card could easily handle a variety of functions, from ATM access to EFTPoS and on to more

specialized functions, such as personal information storage (particularly medical information – a smart card could save lives by providing doctors with a complete medical record of an individual, which could be immediately accessed if that individual were ever admitted to hospital) and access to communications systems. Already, in France, all telephone cards used in France Telecom public payphones are rudimentary smart cards that contain a single microchip.

4. **The smart card as electronic wallet**
   The smart card can be 'loaded' with what are in effect a quantity of spending opportunities, which can then he 'spent' by passing the card through a suitable device. Again, the near-impossibility of copying a smart card means that this application is exceptionally secure, even foolproof. Indeed, this property of the smart card may one day make a huge impact on the entire retail and financial services business, giving card holders the opportunity to keep a secure, personalized, supply of electronic 'cash' in their pockets. Such cash could even be taken abroad without any need for intermediate currency conversion. Clearly, deploying such cards could offer a financial institution the opportunity to gain an enduring competitive edge over its rivals.

The potential offered by these four applications will provide the driving force behind deployment of smart cards, but it may well be that the most important driving force will turn out to be the need to combat the ever-increasing level of plastic card-based fraud within the financial sector. The ability of the smart card to carry out multiple functions is also very attractive. In the US, it is estimated that the average card-carrying person has seven cards. The possibility, if different institutions can agree on a workable sharing agreement, to incorporate many, or all, of these cards into one card will undoubtedly encourage card users to favour the smart card.

THE LIKELY PROGNOSIS OF SMART CARDS

At first, adoption of the smart card is likely to be restrained by its cost, but prices will fall as the technology matures, leading to faster adoption and the benefits of high volume manufacture. Intitially the card will probably penetrate areas where the price is not too critical. For instance, in the US it is estimated that 18 million people are already paying over $50 a year for prestigious gold cards and the cost of the smart card will not be a restriction in this market.

As with all types of banking technology, smart cards will only come into their own when the market-place wants them. However, financial institutions in many countries are poised to start giving the market-place the opportunity to sample the cards. Numerous trials of smart cards are underway through-out the world: in the UK, US, France, Japan, Norway and even Senegal. France has witnessed the greatest progress: smart cards there are becoming universally accepted as a new form of plastic card, although even France has a long way to go before the full potential of smart cards within its retail financial sector can be realized.

THE DALLINGTON COUNTRY CLUB SMART CARD PROJECT

In the UK, one of the most interesting smart card trials to date has been the Barclaycard Visa-sponsored trial at the Dallington Country Club, Northamptonshire, where Visa successfully deployed a smart card payment, information storage and membership authentication system for about 2000 card holders. In May 1991 Visa handed over the pilot project to the Dallington Country Club, where the project has become a permanent part of the Club's operation.

THE 'SUPER-SMART' CARD

A further extension of the smart card concept is the currently experimental 'super-smart card' which is essentially a smart card with input buttons which resembles a credit card sized pocket calculator. The super-smart card, which is being tested in the UK by several suppliers of electronic cards, will allow the card holder to input a variety of personal data into his or her own card. A super-smart card, perhaps used in conjunction with a telephone banking facility or a home banking terminal, may one day be used by customers to create what is almost the equivalent of a bank branch in the customer's own living room. Such a system could even be connected directly to the in-house EFTPoS systems of the main retailers used by the card holder, thereby allowing for goods to be ordered and paid for from the customer's own home.

Such a scenario belongs more to the early part of the twenty-first century than the latter part of the twentieth. But the electronic payment systems revolution has only really got underway in the past ten years or so. Who knows at this stage exactly how far it will go, and in what exciting new consumer-oriented technological applications it will manifest itself?

GUIDELINES FOR WINNING NEW CUSTOMERS WITH SMART CARDS

Tentatively, these guidelines should be seen to be as follows.

1. Unless you are prepared to risk substantial sums in speculative development, do not deploy smart cards until widespread interest in them among other financial institutions indicates that they have entered the growth phase of electronic payment system deployment.
2. As with all types of electronic payment system, be quite certain about the benefits of smart cards to your customers before you start to deploy them.
3. To test these benefits, opt to deploy smart cards on an

experimental basis within a pilot scheme before moving on to a more widespread development.

4. Remember that the history of successful electronic payment systems has shown that – as with ATMS, particularly – an electronic payment system is only truly successful when it appeals to customers across all social and economic classes. Beware of launching a smart card application which appeals purely to higher income groups.

5. There may be important advantages to be gained from deploying smart cards or super-smart cards in conjunction with a telephone banking system, to give customers maximized control over their bank acounts. Bear this in mind when examining possible deployments.

6. Because they can hold far more information about customers than ordinary magnetic stripe cards can, smart cards may offer you the opportunity to target your marketing of other services to customers far more effectively. Exploit this opportunity where it arises, but bear in mind that your customer data storage will probably need to comply with relevant national data protection laws.

7. As inherently glamorous and exciting devices, smart cards, and particularly super-smart cards, obviously have great marketing appeal to customers. As and when you do come round to deploying these advanced cards, take advantage of the inherent glamour of the cards to give a maximum impact to marketing activity based upon them.

CHAPTER SIX

Bringing an electronic payment system to market

INTRODUCTION

The process of bringing a new type of electronic payment system to market represents one of the most interesting challenges facing a retail banking professional. This chapter looks at the most effective method of initiating and managing this launch.

In today's retail banking environment, any new type of payment system launched by an institution will almost always have an important electronic element. However, it is rare that the institution will launch what is purely an electronic payment system. Therefore, with few exceptions, the electronic payment system will usually be launched as part of a new product 'package'. Typically, this new product will include the following elements:

◆   cheque book;
◆   plastic card (and PIN);
◆   interest on credit balances (although this will not necessarily apply to current accounts);
◆   access to an electronic payment system, such as an ATM network, an EFTPoS network, and perhaps also to a telephone banking or other home banking system.

An institution will not usually bring an electronic payment system to market in isolation for the very good reason that giving a customer access to such a system is not of itself likely to be very attractive; what the customer really wants is an entire payment and deposit facility in which the access to the electronic payment system is an essential part of what is being offered, but not all of what is on offer.

Consequently, this chapter focuses on the bringing to market of what is termed 'an initiative', rather than purely an electronic payment system. It will, in any case, be clear from the text that the initiative is likely to include access to an electronic payment system. However, if the institution wants the new initiative to succeed in the market-place, it can hardly expect the electronic payment system alone to attract customers. Since the types of electronic system that are likely to be part of the overall package will either be in the maturity phase of development, or else approaching this phase, it follows that most rival institutions will also be able to give their customers access to the payment system. Consequently, the onus is on the institution to produce a packaged product – incorporating the electronic system – which is attractive to customers, and profitable for the institution.

THE ALBION MUTUAL BUILDING SOCIETY

The Albion Mutual Building Society does not exist, but it is useful for the purposes of the analysis in this chapter to hypothesize a financial institution which is renowned for its expertize in planning and launching new developments. The Albion Mutual is now embarking on a process which will lead it to launch a new current account based around an ATM and EFTPoS facility.

The Albion Mutual's exemplary efforts will be used as a paradigm of how a development and deployment campaign for a retail financial institution's new initiative ought ideally to be carried out. Regrettably, in real life the process of the launch never runs quite as smoothly as it does at the Albion Mutual. However, this excellent institution has a lesson to offer all of us. A UK institution is chosen for convenience.

Why a building society? It is obviously necessary that this

hypothetical institution belongs to one particular category of retail financial institution, and during the past ten years or so UK building societies have definitely displayed more initiative than UK banks in deploying electronic payment systems as part of a marketing initiative. Which is not, of course, to imply that they will always have the edge over banks and other types of institutions in this respect. So, no bias in favour of building societies' likely future success in managing marketing initiatives is intended here.

The stages of the marketing process

Stage one Preparatory planning

Introduction

It sounds obvious, but a plan to launch a new initiative must naturally start somewhere. Furthermore, the origins of the scheme will in many cases suggest how the scheme ought to develop. Few plans to launch initiatives materialize in a fully formed state out of nothing, even if they are being hastily – and most probably ill-advisedly – conceived in order to prevent the institution from falling behind a principal competitor. The Albion Mutual is very wary of such 'automatic response' types of planning, and believes that the eventual launch of its initiative will only be successful if the initiative is, from the outset, in profound harmony with the institution's overall commercial and operational strategy. What the Albion Mutual desires to avoid at all costs is the launch of an initiative which is basically irrelevant to the Society's strategy and achievements to date.

The need to evolve a strategy

The Albion Mutual certainly does not consider that merely responding to a competitor's initiatives by doing what the competing institution is doing is an effective way of starting a strategic process geared towards launching a successful initiative of its own. The Society recognizes that what is wanted is not this kind of automatic knee-jerk reaction but the evolution of a starting-point, and accompanying objectives, which harmonize with the institution's overall commercial strategy. The Albion Mutual would go as far as to believe that there is a case for delaying the launch and risking a competitor obtaining an initial edge, rather than rushing the launch process and incurring the far more costly risk of ending up with a system which not only attracts fewer customers than a more thoughtfully-planned initiative might have done, but which also may need to be abandoned in favour of a better system after only a few years.

The planners at the Albion Mutual are well aware of these hazards and are determined not to start the launch process without a thorough evaluation of their own institution's commercial and operational requirements. They realize, too, that they must at this early stage make a fundamental decision: whether their strategy in launching the new payment system will be one of attack or defence.

Attacking and defensive strategies
An attacking strategy is one where the objective is to establish a competitive advantage over rival institutions. A defensive strategy involves minimizing a competitive advantage which a rival institution has gained, or is believed to have gained.

New legislation, such as the UK Building Societies Act, often tends to widen the range of activities in which a financial institution can participate, and thereby create attacking possibilities because it allows institutions to implement types of accounts and payment systems which could not be implemented before. For example, the Building Societies Act allowed building societies to make personal loans, thereby giving them further encouragement to launch new types of accounts which would win customers who might subsequently become loan customers. However, exciting though the possibilities created by new legislation may be, no institution should automatically assume that it must therefore take advantage of the legislation, just as the emergence of a new type of technology does not mean that an institution must therefore take every step to offer a payment system based on the new technology to its customers. The need for strategic research remains just as strong, and deploying such research usually help an institution to avoid a lemming-like rush into new market areas where it does not really belong.

Just as an attacking strategy must not be allowed to be innovative for its own sake, so a defensive strategy should not be allowed to deteriorate into the planning of a mere copycat version of the rival institution's system. In practical terms, both types of strategy require the same degree of forward planning, although arriving at a decision regarding whether it is an attacking or defensive strategy that is being planned is an important way of defining the fundamental nature of the strategy. For many financial institutions nowadays, the attacking/defensive decision is in effect a way of formulating an answer to the question: 'Are we going to remain entrenched in our traditional market sectors or are we going to expand into new sectors?'. There is nothing necessarily wrong with an institution remaining entrenched in traditional market sectors, if these are generating sufficient profits, but most institutions today are forever seeking ways of expanding into new, profitable market sectors.

An obvious example is the objective of attracting more young customers. The building societies doubtless felt, and were probably right to feel this, that their traditional image was of a secure place where people who were middle-aged in spirit if not in fact could invest funds, and obtain mortgages. During the past decade the building societies have in the main been successful in changing their images towards that of more youth-orientated organizations, although it might be argued that some societies have achieved this objective at the expense of part of their credibility among older account holders.

The need to decide on the profile of the institution
The extent to which a particular institution will want to position itself as a purveyor of financial services to a youthful or older generation of account holders will, of course, vary from institution to institution. The important point to make here is that a decision regarding the institution's own preference on

this matter is exactly the type of strategic decision which must be made as part of the initial planning of an initiative. At the Albion Mutual, which insists on in-depth preparatory planning of all major initiatives, preliminary work on the launch of a new initiative based around a new type of electronic payment system-related product or service involves the institution in the need to obtain detailed answers to the following questions, and ones similar to these.

◆ What are our main areas of business now?
◆ What are likely to be our main areas of business in five, and ten, years from now?
◆ What kind of payment services are we offering our customers now?
◆ What kind of payment services do we want to be offering our customers in five, and ten, years from now?
◆ What is our motivation for becoming involved in a new payment system?
◆ Are we all right as we are? If not, why not?
◆ Are we big enough for our new payment system to make a real impact on the market?
◆ Can we afford to change?

If, and only if, the answers to these questions suggest that it is in the interests of the institution's strategic aims to consider developing a new payment system – whether this be a new type of account or a new level of participation in an electronic payments network – the Albion Mutual will proceed to the next stage of decision-making: the need to define the requirements of the system.

Stage two Defining the system's requirements

Introduction

The purpose of this stage of the research process is to specify what the system should achieve for the institution, and thereby start clarifying what kind of system it should be, and within what parameters it will operate. At this stage, it may well become clear that the solution required by the institution is not simply a new level of participation in an electronic system, but rather a new type of account facility that offers an important electronic element.

Perhaps the greatest danger facing an institution here is that the institution may make an unduly hasty decision regarding what type of system is required, and will – either consciously or unconsciously – arrange for its research to furnish the conclusions that it wants to see. 'Research' of this nature is of course all too common within the business world, where research can be made to justify almost any kind of pre-specialized conclusion. However, for a financial institution which is considering embarking on a major marketing initiative that will not only cost a great deal of money but also commit it to a particular type of marketing strategy for several years hence, hastening the research phase in order to push home a preconceived conclusion can be disastrous.

The three stages of research

At the Albion Mutual, research into defining the requirements of the system takes place at three principal levels.

Firstly, every effort is made to provide an accurate profile of the existing customer base. This involves looking at such factors as geographic distribution of the customer base; demographic considerations, such as the average age at which people become account holders; and examining detailed information regarding the current take-up of all the institution's services, from mortgages to loans and deposit accounts.

Secondly, the institution conducts market research to find out what type of new service is likely to be most successful, both in terms of meeting the needs of existing customers and wooing new ones. 'Market research' is a blanket term, much beloved of advertising agencies. Good market research within the retail financial sector is unfortunately much less easy to obtain than many advertising agencies believe. Although there is certainly a great deal to be said for conducting formal market research into customers' needs, it is likely that much of the most rewarding feedback will be gained from branch-based members of staff who should have a good knowledge of what their customers want. In any case, market research is notoriously bad at predicting future changes in customers' wishes. Some element of prediction will therefore be inevitable when planning the new system. The emphasis, however, should be on reducing the uncertainty factor to a minimum.

In general, institutions can take comfort from the observation that retail customers the world over have shown that they are almost always prepared to change their retail banking habits and use new types of accounts featuring electronic payment facilities, if the new account offers them more convenience and a wider choice of payment method. We can usefully bear in mind the story in Chapter Two of the early days of ATMs, and recall that ATMs only came into their own when ATM cards were made available to the widest range of people – including blue-collar workers who could not easily get to a bank during the week. If a new account facility or payment system offers customers more convenience, then other things being equal it is likely to prove successful. What an institution must above all guard against is a naïve assessment of the benefits which a possible new account or system will offer. It cannot be repeated too often that innovation for its own sake is very likely to prove disastrous for the institution succumbing to the temptation to place innovation first and foremost. But make added convenience your touchstone, and success is likely to be within your grasp.

The third type of research is the most immediately pragmatic. The Albion Mutual conducts a careful examination of the means available to implement a new payment system. Although one would expect that an institution could provide much of the expertise required to project manage the implementation from within its own staff, it is inevitable that many elements of the new system or account will need to be 'bought in' from outside. Fortunately, an institution looking to launch a new payment system in the 1990s has an array of suppliers to choose from, whereas if the institution was carrying out the launch twenty years or so ago, it would have had to improvise far more of the elements.

Examples of the types of external suppliers whose expertise would be necessary to implement any proposed system are:

hardware suppliers
network operators
software engineers
computer security consultants
plastic card manufacturers
chequebook manufacturers
designers
branding agencies
advertising agencies
public relations consultancies
credit card account management organizations
customer account management organizations.

Managing the supplier relationship
The range of opportunities for an institution to delegate its requirements is, as the above list suggests, quite astonishing, and while there must be few institutions which would be prepared to delegate a function as commercially intimate as customer account management, institutions will certainly find it reassuring to reflect that by careful selection of suppliers they should be able to avoid weak links in their post-launch business activities. Certainly, the range of suppliers available to retail institutions is wide enough for an institution to be able to delegate to an external supplier almost any aspect of launching and operating the new account and system. For some institutions, which are relatively unpractised in spearheading a major marketing initiative of this type, the range of outside expertise to choose from may become bewildering. It is necessary for an institution to keep its corporate feet on the ground, and decide from the outset that it is going to be fully in control of its suppliers, and not be mastered by them. It is all too easy, when confronted with external specialists who seem to know what they are talking about, to assume that they know all the answers and that the institution's own hard-won expertise counts for nothing.

In fact, there are very few exceptions to the rule that the dominating motive behind the advice which a specialist organization provides (with the exception perhaps, of specialists in the caring professions) **is, first and foremost, to generate additional business for the specialist**. If this sounds an overly cynical viewpoint, consider how likely it would be for an advertising agency, if approached by an institution regarding the launch of a new type of retail account, to suggest that a public relations campaign would be cheaper and more convenient. Similarly, no supplier of mainframe computers is going to point out that a minicomputer, or even a local area network powered by a personal computer, would discharge a task equally well, and at much lower costs.

This is a necessary warning, but no institution worth its deposits should approach possible suppliers from anything other than a position of what one might term courteous cynicism. Indeed, I suspect that most suppliers prefer to work with clients who know in broad terms where they are going and what they want. Again, I would emphasize the need for an institution to research the requirements of its implementation long before it begins to investigate ways of carrying the implementation through.

Above all, the huge advantage which an institution has is that all external suppliers are very keen to work with financial institutions, whom they consider (rightly, one hopes), to be creditworthy, and liable to spend relatively large sums of money on the final implementation. They also hope that the successful completion of one project will lead to the opportunity to participate in another.

Since the institution's business is so important to suppliers, it is reasonable for the institution to ask different suppliers for an exact breakdown of what they could provide in terms of external assistance, and for an accurate estimate of the costs that would be involved in discharging a particular element of the implementation process. Using these estimates, the institution should be able to produce reasonably accurate budget estimates for various implementation options. Suppliers should also be asked within what time frame they can provide the services for which they are quoting, and these time frames ought to form part of any contract which the institution enters into with the supplier.

The need to take time over the three phases

The three phases of research in Stage two seem clear enough, but they should not be hurried. The Albion Mutual spent more than a year over Stage two, defining a strategy that was in harmony with the wishes of the institution's customers; looking at the various types of implementation possibilities and examining what types of external suppliers would be necessary to put the different implementations into practice. Finally, the nature of the project was decided upon. The Albion Mutual elected to implement a new type of current account, one that carried a debit card which could be used in a variety of ATMs, as well as in an EFTPoS system.

Stage three Gathering the tools of implementation

Introduction

Stage three involves the process of an institution finalizing its plans for what it wants to do and assembling the different tools which it will use in order to achieve its objectives.

Many of these tools will be supplied by external organizations because it is unlikely that an institution would have the necessary degree of expertise in-house. One obvious reason for this is that some of the services are highly specialized, and it would be uneconomic for an institution to try to develop such a specialized capability itself. This is not to say, however, that the institution will not be able to provide certain elements of expertise in-house, particularly since it is likely to be much cheaper to supply some elements from inside rather than going to external suppliers, who will naturally factor their profits into their charges, in addition to the cost of actually supplying the services. Advertising and marketing, for example, might be managed by an in-house team, and some of the data processing workload arising from a proposed new electronic payment system might be handled by the institution's own computer systems department. However, there are also positive benefits in using external specialists. Making use of in-house resources will only be less expensive if the institution already has its own expertise in place, otherwise using an outside supplier will almost certainly be far cheaper than setting up an in-house department from scratch. In any case, a retail financial institution should focus on doing what it does best; that is, running customer accounts and thinking up new ways to improve its market share.

Another big advantage of using external suppliers is that, being specialists, they are likely to be able to bring their resources to bear on an institution's behalf very quickly. Indeed, if they are unable to do this, they should not be used.

Once the institution has decided which functions it wishes to carry out and which it intends to delegate to an external supplier, the process of selecting external suppliers can begin in earnest. Beyond suggesting that the process should focus on the three principal criteria of the quality, cost and timeliness of the external supply, it would be inadvisable to lay down the law on how an institution should select its suppliers, simply because all institutions will have differing requirements, but it should certainly be said that time spent on the selection process will certainly be repaid in that by selecting the best supplier(s) for the job, the implementation process will go more smoothly and in the long (or short) run save time.

Testing the mettle of suppliers

The Albion Mutual had the excellent idea of using the launch of its new current account as a means of testing the mettle of its existing advertising agency and public relations consultancy. During the period of time allocated to the selection process the Albion Mutual's advertising and public relations accounts came up for review, and the Society decided to invite several other advertising agencies and public relations consultancies to pitch for the business by asking them to suggest strategies for the launch of the new current account. Such competitive pitches are common throughout the marketing world. Once the review had been completed, the Society was well placed to decide which advertising agency and public relations consultancy would be most likely to handle its business successfully. The society also had a number of alternative strategies from which to choose. It should, however, be said that it is not very ethical for an institution to test suppliers' nettle in this way unless it is genuinely considering changing its supplies. Furthermore, in order to be fair, a constitution really ought to make a payment to any of the suppliers whose ideas it used without appointing the supplier in question.

Generating a list of preferred suppliers

The ultimate purpose of this third stage is to generate a list of preferred suppliers with whose aid the institution can reasonably expect to initiate, complete and manage the implementation within a specified time period.

Stage four Implementation

Introduction

The three previous stages having been satisfactorily completed, the institution can move on to the implementation phase.

Even though the preliminary research has suggested the type of new account or payment system that the institution should deploy, and even though the list of suppliers has been compiled, the actual implementation process can only proceed when the institution's Board of Directors has examined a specific recommendation, and has opted to act on this. It is important to note that during the research and supplier selection process, the parameters which led to the original plan may have changed and the plan may itself need to be enhanced or otherwise modified prior to the implementation proceeding. No institution should ever move to the implementation phase without being aware of all such factors which may have moved the goalposts, and which may indeed move them during the phase. Particularly where the electronic payment facility will be an important part of the new initiative, major factors may alter within only a few months. For example, an ATM network to which the institution intended to connect its own ATMs may have merged with another network, or an EFTPoS system that was previously a market leader may (as in the sad case of EftPoS UK) have ceased operations, or simply lost its dominant market share.

However, assuming that the implementation can go ahead as planned, or that it can go ahead after some modifications, the institution will be able to proceed to the task of managing the implementation.

Managing the implementation

Although there are many consultancies which are well able to undertake the management of almost any kind of retail banking project, I am firmly convinced that an institution should manage its own project unless there are very good reasons to the contrary, such as when a small institution is becoming involved in a major new initiative and does not have any in-house staff with expertise in managing the implementation of the initiative. However, even in this case the institution would be well-advised to supervise the work in the closest detail.

What the institution wants, above all, is control of the implementation. In order to ensure that this is achieved, the institution should draw up a 'critical path' which includes all the significant tasks that must be completed.

In the case of the Albion Mutual and its new current account, these include:

◆ staff training and preparation of staff instruction manuals;
◆ planning the specifications of the account;
◆ planning the implementation of related electronic systems and any necessary switching;
◆ cheque book design and production;
◆ plastic card design and production;
◆ researching and branding the new account;
◆ planning and implementing the marketing campaign;
◆ planning and implementing the launch campaign;
◆ planning and implementing the promotion and management of the account after the launch.

At every stage of this process the research that was gathered earlier in the planning process will naturally come into its own. Again, many (or even all) of the elements in the critical path could be delegated to a specialized consultancy. However, the institution itself should in almost every case retain to itself the task of co-ordinating the entire project and bringing the disparate elements together.

Costing the new initiative
Any new initiative in the retail banking sector will inevitably involve the creation of a corresponding new infrastructure. The infrastructure will consist of a variety of elements; in particular the construction or (which is more likely) connection to the new electronic systems, all the other practicalities relating to implementing the initiative, and the retraining of existing or newly-recruited staff who will carry out the implementation. Building the new infrastructure will naturally cost a relatively large amount of money, and it is usually unrealistic for an institution to expect to make a profit on the initiative before at least three years have elapsed. In most cases, institutions tend to take a five-year viewpoint on a major new initiative, and would only expect the initiative to go into profit after five years, although a well-researched and well-planned initiative should from the outset bring the institution considerable benefits in terms of new account holders and an increased profile in the market-place. The extent of these benefits – and of the subsequent profits – will, of course, depend on the wisdom and resourcefulness that the institution has deployed when planning and implementing the system.

Detailed and realistic budgetary forecasts of how the new initiative is expected to impact on the institution's overall revenue and profits must be drawn up once the precise nature of the initiative is known. Even the most professionally run and best managed institutions are sometimes susceptible to over optimism here, and it is preferable to err on the side of caution, particularly in terms of how a new type of account will increase revenue from deposits. A new type of account that meets a real need in the market-place will always find its public, but customers may need time to become fully aware of it, especially since word of mouth is an important way in which information about a new account spreads.

Accommodating opportunity cost

Although the cost of buying in external resources, such as consultancy services and bureau facilities, can usually be easily ascertained, some institutions fail fully to appreciate the need for performing a related costing process based on the 'opportunity cost' of diverting in-house resources to the new initiative. Opportunity cost is the cost which represents the financial benefits which those diverted resources could have brought to the institution if they had not been diverted. It is important to make the conceptual distinction between costing in-house resources according to the principle of opportunity cost instead of simply basing the cost on what the resource actually costs the institution. This is a particularly important distinction to make when assessing the cost of diverting a member of staff to the new initiative. A member of staff might cost the institution £X per month in terms of salary and national insurance, but bring the institution, say, £4X during a month in terms of productivity. It is clear that the true cost of diverting that person to the new initiative for one month is not £X but £4X, and the costing of the new initiative should be based on this latter sum. Similarly, if a particular computer system is expected to generate revenue for an institution of £1 million over a three-month period, the true cost of diverting that computer to the new initiative for three months is the £1 million in lost revenue, not the three-monthly cost of depreciation and lost interest which the computer 'costs' the institution. Of course, it is very likely – and should become more likely as time goes on – that the resources diverted to the new initiative may soon bring the institution additional sources of revenue. The point is, however, that the correct way to cost the diverted resources is to base the budget upon opportunity cost.

Marketing the new initiative

Marketing the new initiative has been mentioned above on several occasions. Inevitably, marketing the new initiative cannot be considered in isolation but must harmonize with every stage of the initiative's development. The initiative must be planned from the outset with marketing in mind, just as the marketing process needs to fit in with the principal aims of the initiative.

As has already been suggested, planning a marketing campaign for a new initiative is an excellent opportunity for an institution to review service providers such as its advertising agency and public relations consultancy. Ideally, these service providers should be asked to prepare plans of activity for each of three fundamentally different approaches to the marketing task.

The marketing options

The first approach would be a campaign directed at giving the new initiative a very high profile as a remarkable innovation in retail banking and a completely new departure for the institution concerned.

The second approach would position the initiative as an important enhancement of the institution's range of services, but not a radical new departure.

The third approach would be a low-profile campaign that introduced the initiative as a continuation of the institution's existing service.

The agency or consultancy making the three different proposals should suggest which of the three approaches it considers most appropriate. Advertising agencies and public relations consultancies tend to favour high-profile types of campaigns – since these lead to higher media spends or greater consultancy time allocations – **what matters is not the splash which a marketing campaign makes, but the breadth and duration of the ripples**. Although many new initiatives are launched with a major high-profile advertising and public relations campaign, such an approach is by no means always necessary, even where an institution is launching an important new account of its own. For example, the Albion Mutual, which draws most of its customer base at present from the Midlands, decided against a major national marketing campaign when it launched its new current account but opted for a more modest promotion based on mailings to existing customers, press advertising in the leading daily and weekly Midlands papers, and some radio advertising.

The decision as to which type of campaign is most appropriate should not be taken lightly. Not only is a considerable sum of marketing money at stake, but an institution's own investors and deposit holders are only too well aware of how expensive high-profile advertising can be, and are apt to be highly critical of advertising which they feel to be misdirected. For example, the directors of one major UK building society came under intense pressure during the Society's 1991 Annual General Meeting from members who felt that a controversial high-profile television advertisement, which the Society had been running, was pretentious and ineffective. During the meeting one of the directors admitted that he did not like the advertising, but argued that the best test of advertising was not whether people liked it, but whether or not it would be remembered. He was, in effect, saying that there is no such thing as bad publicity. This viewpoint is, to put it mildly, questionable, and has the unmistakable ring of 'adagencyspeak' about it. Advertising agencies are only too happy to persuade clients that a high-profile campaign is bound to succeed in any event, since even if customers and potential customers do not like the advertising they will at least remember the name of the advertiser. Such an attitude may well be true when the products being advertised are fast-moving consumer goods (fmcg), such as chocolate bars or washing-powder, where instantaneous customer recognition is obviously of great importance, but a financial institution's services and products are a different matter, and it seems likely that a misjudged high-profile advertising campaign can cause an institution a great deal of damage. In this context it is certainly relevant to point out that the day or two after the AGM mentioned above was reported in the UK's *The Independent* newspaper, a letter appeared in the paper in which the writer said that the next time she had funds to deposit in a building society, she would be careful to avoid societies that were spending money on ineffective advertisements. Such a sentiment is very likely widespread among the general public.

The need for a wide definitional approach to marketing

It is by no means necessary for marketing to be restricted to advertising and public relations. The requirements of the marketing campaign should inspire every aspect of the new initiative, from the branding of the new product to the design of the elements that the public will handle and/or see, and on to the actual means by which the initiative is launched. However, provided that the initiative has been well-researched and well-planned from the beginning, it is unlikely that there will be any difficulty in the institution harmonizing the marketing of the new account or system with the overall implementation process.

Branding

The sad fact is that financial institutions often get branding wrong, and suffer lost custom and unachieved revenue and profits as a consequence.

There are two main reasons for this. First, financial institutions often display extraordinary naïvity in terms of the brand names which they select for their products. Perhaps the most naïve aspect of their thinking is their automatic assumption that their cunningly-designed products and systems necessarily need an unusual branding. I will return to this point in a moment.

Secondly, and this point is closely connected with the first, institutions pay too much heed to the branding-related advice of advertising agencies or specialized brand-name consultancies. Almost all the experience which advertising agencies and specialists have gained on the subject of branding has been gained with fast-moving consumer goods. Concocting a brand name for a new type of biscuit is one thing; branding a new type of bank account in which a customer might be invited to invest many thousands of pounds is quite another. Surely, when considering a branding, a financial institution is better off relying on its own lengthy experience of supplying retail financial services to its clients than relying on the experience of an agency which has little or no proven expertise in devising brandings which attract customers?

When faced with the necessity to brand a new product or system, an institution has three principal options.

1. Firstly, it can employ a 'customized name' which has been plucked from some other, non-financial, area of human activity, normally an area with agreeable overtones. Examples of this are 'Visa', which of course comes from the world of international travel; Midland Bank's 'Orchard', 'Meridien' and 'Vector' accounts, which sound rather as if they were coined by branding specialists; and the UK EFTPoS system 'Switch'.

   The trouble with customized brand names is that they simply might not be attractive to customers, and whereas an unsuccessful chocolate bar or washing powder can easily be rethought, rebranded and relaunched, a financial institution will hardly have the opportunity to make such a revision. There is a great onus on the institution to get the branding right first time. True, Visa and Switch are brands that have succeeded very well, but perhaps this is less due to the branding than to the fact that they were both highly innovative propositions (an international credit card chain and a national EFTPoS system). If an individual institution is launching a new product which is unlikely to be quite as innovative as Visa and Switch, there is a real danger that a customized name will fall flat on its face due to the fact that it is solely a brand name and so can itself convey little, or nothing, about the nature of the product.

   There is ample evidence within the financial sector that too many institutions choose customized brandings without really considering whether this is the best option for them. Probably they feel that their new product is far too nice and attractive to be given a name which roots it firmly in the mundane world of finance. Visa and Switch are brand names that certainly mean something in their own right. However, if an institution chooses a name that does not have any particular connotation relating to the product on offer it runs the grave risk that it may not only find that the name fails to make a coherent sales message, but may also find that the name confuses customers regarding what the new product actually is.

Another problem connected with using a customized branding has already been touched upon. Almost by definition, a new type of financial account is going to have a lengthy life; at least ten years, and perhaps much longer. During that period of time the effectiveness of the branding may have worn out completely. Tastes for different brandings also vary considerably between account holders from different countries, and the growing internationalization of the financial sector (particular with the Single European Market of 1992 in mind) means that the different tastes of account holders from different countries cannot easily be ignored. In the US, for example, there is a fondness for naming ATM networks in a rather gaudy fashion ('Magic Line' and the 'New York Cash Exchange' are two examples), whereas in the UK retail financial sector brandings tend to be more conservative.

One can only conclude that a financial institution which opts for a customized branding runs a real risk of opening a can of worms. It is reasonable to ask whether the risk is really necessary?

2. The second option is that the institution uses what I call a 'compound branding', since it is normally formed by combining two elements that have a meaning when used individually, and can be given a proprietary meaning when combined. Examples are the Halifax Building Society's 'CardCash' account, Barclays Bank's 'Barclaycard' and the Nationwide Building Society's 'FlexAccount'.

A compound branding may not superficially be as attractive as a customized branding, but it has the prime advantage of being a relatively safe option, since it can usually be made to convey exactly what a new account or system is all about much more easily than can a customized branding; customized brandings usually being restricted to conveying meaning by association.

3. The third option is for an institution to plump for what I might call the 'logical branding' option. This is simply a matter of branding the new account or system with a name that describes exactly what it is. In fact, the Albion Mutual decided to call its new current account, 'Current Account', thus avoiding any problems with choosing a customized or compound branding which caused ambiguities. Despite choosing a safe, unadventurous name, the Albion Mutual created a stylish design to go with the branding, and were very satisfied with the take-up of the new account both among both existing and new customers. The Society felt, very likely with good reason, that its customers appreciated the directness and lack of pretension of the branding. The Society chose a youthful but sober design for the plastic card, cheque book and account literature.

Stage five Post-implementation

Introduction
It should hardly be necessary to point out that an institution's work does not come to an end once the new initiative is in place. A concerted and consistent programme of post-implementation monitoring is essential in order to ensure that the benefits of the initiative to the institution – and to its customers – are maximized.

The need for monitoring
Two particular areas will need to be the focus of the monitoring process are:

1. the take-up of the initiative among customers;
2. the initiative's perceived profile.

Both these areas can be monitored; the first on a purely in-house basis, the second by gaining information from staff who deal with customers and also perhaps from market research organizations. Feedback on these key areas will help to define the kind of post-implementation supporting activity in which the institution should participate. Information regarding the take-up of the initiative among customers may, for example, suggest improved ways for the sales message to be conveyed to potential new customers. Information regarding the perceived profile of the new initiative might suggest the nature of follow-up advertising.

Both these principal types of monitoring criterion are, of course, related. For example, in the case of the Albion Mutual the Society found, at the end of the first year after implementation, that its new 'Current Account' had gained significant new business among customers aged up to 35, but had fared less well among older customers. The Society concluded that one reason for this was that the vast majority of its staff who dealt with new account queries were themselves youthful, and consequently suitable interlocutors for younger people who were planning on switching to the new account, but less appropriate for the Society's older range of customers. As a result of this post-implementation activity, the Albion Mutual decided to take two major steps. First, it increased the proportion of new account staff who were in their forties and fifties, and it planned and implemented a post-launch advertising campaign which was specifically designed to appeal to older customers.

SUMMARY

The retail financial sector is increasingly competitive. This is in part due to the breakdown of demarcation barriers between different types of institutions (e.g. in the UK, building societies can now provide a full banking service), and partly due to international agreements (particularly between members of the European Community) allowing more intensive cross-border competition. Within this increasingly competitive scenario, the role of new products and services – new customer-winning and profit-generating initiatives of all kind – has never been more important. It is vital to the prosperity of a retail financial institution in both the long and short term that it can research, plan, implement and manage such new initiatives, especially those which involve customers being offered the all important resources of electronic payment systems.

This chapter has frequently emphasized the need to plan a new initiative carefully and the dangers of launching an initiative merely in order to copy a rival institution's initiative. It seems reasonable to reiterate the requirement of careful planning: thus ensuring that the launch of any initiative is in harmony with the institution's overall strategic and commercial objectives, and also maximizing the likelihood that the initiative will appeal to customers. If both these conditions of planning and public acceptance are met, there is every chance that the institution's own contribution towards the electronic payment systems revolution will – like all revolutions which are well-planned and are backed by the people – score a resounding success.

Finally, to end this chapter, here is a checklist of the different questions that must be addressed by an institution planning to launch a new initiative featuring an electronic payment system, where the institution wishes to maximize the effectiveness of the launch from start to finish.

CHECKLIST OF QUESTIONS TO ADDRESS WHEN PLANNING, LAUNCHING AND MARKETING A NEW ELECTRONIC PAYMENT SERVICE-RELATED INITIATIVE

◆ Do we require an attacking strategy (i.e. is our objective to establish a competitive advantage over rival institutions)?
◆ Do we require a defensive strategy (i.e. is our objective to minimize a competitive advantage which a rival institution has gained)?
◆ Have we recognized the danger of being innovative for its own sake?

- Have we recognized the danger of developing a mere copy-cat version of a rival institution's initiative?
- Have we recognized the danger of the new development appealing to younger customers at the expense of older customers?
- What are our main areas of business now?
- What are likely to be our main areas of business five, and ten, years from now?
- What kind of payment services are we offering our customers now?
- What kind of payment services do we want to be offering our customers five, and ten, years from now?
- What is our motivation for becoming involved in a new payment system?
- Are we all right as we are? If not, why not?
- Are we big enough for our new payment system to make a real impact on the market?
- Can we afford to change?
- What is the nature of our existing customer base?
- What type of new initiative is likely to appeal to the widest range of those customers?
- Will the new initiative genuinely offer customers added convenience and flexibility in their access to banking systems?
- Which external suppliers will we need?
- Are we approaching external consultants in a calmly cynical frame of mind?
- Do we have acceptable costings for the new initiative?
- Have we accommodated the opportunity cost of diverting resources to the new initiative?
- Are we going to stay on budget?
- How will we market the new initiative?
- Have we assembled a list of preferred suppliers?
- Have we devised a workable and realistic branding?
- Have we planned, in detail, the specifications of the new initiative?
- Have we planned the implementation of related electronic systems and any necessary switching?

- Have we organized cheque book design and production (if applicable)?
- Have we organized plastic card design and production (if applicable)?
- Have we organized the marketing campaign?
- Have we organized the launch campaign?
- Have we organized the post-launch promotion and management of the account?
- Have we arranged staff training?
- Have we arranged for the preparation of staff training manuals?

CHAPTER SEVEN

Electronic payment systems in action

This chapter provides information relating to the extent of implementation of the major type of electronic payment systems discussed in this book within the following geographical locations:

1. UK;
2. US;
3. Continental Europe (in certain selected countries, i.e. Belgium, France, Germany, The Netherlands, Portugal and Spain).

Unless otherwise stated, all the figures are current as of 31 July 1991.

The three types of electronic payment system to which the statistics relate are Automated Teller Machine (ATMs), Electronic Funds Transfer at Point of Sale (EFTPoS) and Telephone Banking. In addition, details of the extent of smart card implementation are also given, where applicable.

UK

Automated Teller Machines

The UK ATM scene divides neatly into two categories: ATMs operated by the major clearing banks, and ATMs operated by the shared network LINK. The cards of some leading banks can be used in LINK ATMs, but in no other sense can the clearing bank systems and the LINK system be said to share ATMs.

There are two clearing bank networks. One is known by the banks as the 'Four Banks' network, although it is not branded as such. This network has as its members the Bank of Scotland, Barclays Bank, Lloyds Bank and the Royal Bank of Scotland. The other network is known as the 'Mint' network (although, again, it is not branded as such), with its members being the Clydesdale Bank (an associated member), the Midland Bank, the National Westminster Bank and the TSB. Both these networks are perhaps best described as reciprocal arrangements rather than branded networks, since no attempt is made to brand them.

The Four Banks network currently contains about 5900 ATMs, with about 16 million cards issued. The figures for the Mint network are in the vicinity of 7500 ATMs and 17 million cards issued.

LINK is the brand name of the Harrogate-based LINK Interchange Network, the UK's national card network, which provides the only shared, branded ATM network in the UK. LINK operates and maintains its own computer systems which provides the switching service between different institutions' proprietary ATMs, and runs the associated settlement and administrative services to members.

The network was established in 1986, with the first inter-building society transaction taking place in April 1986 and the first building society/bank transaction in February 1987.

The main LINK parameters, as of 31 July 1991, were 5325 ATMs and 19 million card holders. The LINK network is projected to achieve more than 6016 ATMs by the end of 1992, serving 20 million card holders. By 1994, this is projected to reach 6100 ATMs and 28 million cards issued. Systems capacity is already in place to handle a three-fold increase in transactions.

LINK membership is for any reputable organization, and the current membership extends to banks, building societies, other financial organizations and card issuers, such as American Express and Diners Club.

LINK members are divided into two categories: those of 'owner members' and 'non-owner members'. This does not refer to whether or not the institutions own ATMs, as all LINK members do, but to whether or not the member owns part of LINK and attends the LINK Board as a director of the company.

The following organizations are currently owner members of LINK:

Abbey National PLC
Alliance & Leicester Building Society
AIB Bank (N)
Bank of Scotland
Birmingham Midshires Building Society (N)
Bradford & Bingley Building Society
Bristol & West Building Society
Britannia Building Society (N)
Clydesdale Bank
Co-operative Bank
Coventry Building Society (N)
Derbyshire Building Society (N)
Girobank
Halifax Building Society
HFC Bank (N)
Leeds Permanent Building Society
National & Provincial Building Society
Northern Rock Building Society (N)
Nationwide Building Society
Woolwich Building Society
Yorkshire Bank PLC
Yorkshire Building Society (N).

The following organizations are non-owner members of LINK:

Airdrie Savings Bank (N)
American Express Europe (N)

Chelsea Building Society (N)
Citibank/Diners International (N)
Cumberland Building Society (N)
Dunfermline Building Society (N)
North of England Building Society (N)
Norwich & Peterborough Building Society (N)
Portman Building Society (N)
Western Trust Limited (N).

There is also a LINK-certified, privately-owned service bureau, Nexus Payments Systems International, which acts as the point of entry to LINK for all the organizations in the above lists which have (N) appended to their names.

LINK's central computer only 'sees' shared transactions (i.e. conducted by a card holder of one member on an ATM owned by another member), apart from those transactions shared between Nexus customers, marked (N). From an initial monthly shared transaction level of 300 000 in February 1987, the number of shared transactions had risen to 9.6 million during July 1991. This represents an average of 3.58 shared transactions per second during the entire month.

The core services provided via LINK are: cash withdrawal, transaction receipt with balance; balance enquiries; fast cash, enabling speedy access to a fixed amount. LINK machines are available 24 hours a day, 365 days of the year.

Some LINK members are involved in international ATM sharing, being participants in the North American-based international ATM network, PLUS system, which opens up more than 50 000 ATMs in North America, Asia and Australasia. In addition, some individual members of LINK have reciprocal relationships with networks in Spain, Portugal and Belgium, which are operated by Nexus.

Electronic Funds Transfer at Point of Sale

Details of the development of EFTPoS in the UK are given in Chapter Three. The fundamental statistics for the two EFTPoS schemes in the UK, one operated by Visa and the other by Switch, are as follows.

Visa scheme

Visa is primarily a credit card organization in the UK. However, its remit as a payment systems operator also includes EFTPoS. The two major EFTPoS Visa card issuers are Barclays Bank and Lloyds Bank, whose 'Connect' card and Lloyds Bank Payment card are issued to 3.9 million and 3.5 million card holders, respectively. These card holders have access to about 150 000 terminals.

Switch

Switch is an EFTPoS consortium with the following financial institutions as members:

Bank of Scotland
Barclays Bank
Clydesdale Bank/Northern Bank
Halifax Building Society
Midland Bank
National Westminster Bank
Royal Bank of Scotland
Yorkshire Bank.

There are currently about 12 million Switch cards in circulation in the UK, and more than 100 000 terminals. By the end of 1991 Switch anticipates operating about 150 000 terminals.

Telephone banking

Telephone banking is already well-established in the UK (see Table 4.2, p. 74). For the Maxim and FlexAccount services offered by the Halifax and Nationwide Anglia Building Societies, respectively, the brand name refers to an account for which a telephone banking service is an available option.

Smart cards

Although there has been a successful pilot trial of smart cards in the UK by Barclays Bank at the Dallington Country Club (see Chapter Five), Barclays – which is probably the pioneering bank for smart card technology in the UK – has no current plans to extend this scheme into a wider initiative. A source at Barclays Bank told me that the bank was actively interested in examining business opportunities in the financial sector based around the smart card. However, the source emphasized that the bank did not see smart cards as an end in themselves, but rather as part of a payment system, proposals for which would have to be considered on their own merits.

US

Automated Teller Machines

ATMs were invented and pioneered in the US. Although Japan has now superseded the US in terms of ATMs per head of the population (this is principally because of the heavy cultural emphasis in Japan towards paying for goods in cash) the US is still the world's leading innovator in ATM design and implementation. In particular, US financial institutions were the first to 'humanize' ATMs and make them user-friendly, both by maximizing the efficiency of the user-interface in the ATMs' design and also by branding ATM networks in a 'friendly' fashion.

Figure 7.1 shows the increase in the number of ATMs in the US since 1975, the first year for which collective records were kept.

According to the US Electronic Funds Transfer Association, the projected figures for the following four years are as follows:

    1991   84 000
    1992   88 000
    1993   93 000
    1994   98 000.

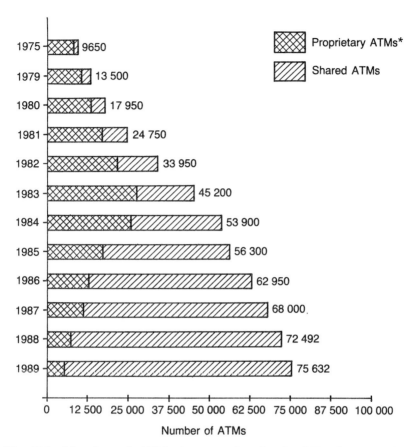

Fig. 7.1 Number of ATMs in operation in the US, showing the number of proprietary and shared ATMs. *Not participating in a shared index. Source: Electronic Funds Transfer Association.

The large population and geographical area of the US, combined with Federal legislation that restricts the operation of banks to a particular State, has led to the creation of the highest number of regional shared ATM networks in the world. There are currently 75 of these, with the main parameters of the top five being as follows (as of the end of September 1991):

1. Star system (California)
   11 901 ATMs; 21.8 million card holders;

2. NYCE (New York/New Jersey)
   10 055 ATMs; 18 million card holders;
3. Honor (Maitland, Florida)
   7904 ATMs; 16 million card holders;
4. MAC (Philadelphia)
   7802 ATMs; 18.3 million card holders;
5. MOST (Virginia)
   4673 ATMs; 8 million card holders.

There are also two US-wide shared networks. These both also have sharing arrangements with overseas networks. CIRRUS gives its 70 million card holders access to 53 000 US-based ATMs and 16 000 overseas ATMs. The Rival network PLUS gives its 175 million card holders access to 43 000 US-based ATMs and 17 600 overseas ATMs.*

Electronic Funds Transfer at Point of Sale

EFTPoS has been part of the US electronic payments scene since 1984, although EFTPoS has not proved particularly popular in the US. The number of terminals which accepted EFTPoS cards in 1990 was about 53 000 – a relatively low figure for a country with a population of around 250 million. In 1990 the total number of EFTPoS transactions in the US was about 12.5 million.

The five leading US EFTPoS schemes, by total transactions in 1990s, are given below. The listing contains the information in the following order: the name of the scheme, the town or city where the scheme has its head office, the number of transactions in 1990, the number of terminals on-line, and the number of cards issued. The figures were current for June 1990.

1. Interlink; San Francisco, CA; 6 million; 12 500; 12 million.
2. Star; San Diego, CA; 1.2 million; 9428; 19.5 million.
3. Cactus; Phoenix, AZ; 810 000; 2825; 1.5 million.

---

*Source of US figures: *Bank Network News*, a leading research organization for US electronic payment schemes.

4. MAC; Philadelphia, PA; 501 000; 9350; 16 million.
5. Pulse; Houston, TX; 480 000; 3200; 8 million.

The names of the EFTPoS schemes ranked from 6 to 10 in order of transaction volumes in 1990 provide further evidence of the tendency of US electronic payment networks to have 'friendly' brands. These networks are: 6. Honor; 7. Exchange/ Accel; 8. Schazam; 9. Owl; 10. Pacific Interchange.

Telephone banking

The last year for which figures are available for telephone banking in the US is 1990. In that year, a survey of 400 banks by the American Bankers Association (ABA) showed that 26% of large banks (i.e. those with more than $1 billion of assets) and 5% of banks with less than $1 billion of assets offered some form of home banking service. These figures represented a considerable increase on 1989, when only 3% of all banks surveyed said that they offered home banking services.

Overall, the trend in the US is that more and more US banks offer electronic services that allow customers to undertake routine banking tasks from home, either using a touch tone telephone or a home computer. According to the ABA, about 85% of banks offering these services either lost money on providing the service or broke even. It is a little puzzling why the ABA has seen fit to focus on this last point, since banks would not normally expect to make a profit by providing home or telephone banking facilities, but would expect that providing this service would allow them to make savings elsewhere, such as within their branches.

Despite the likelihood of a relatively high initial outlay on setting up the telephone banking scheme, US banks are clearly still keen to participate in this. For example, Citibank/Citicorp has spent millions of dollars developing home banking services and devices that will make it easier for customers to do banking from home. Citicorp has been developing a device called the 'Enhanced Telephone', which is basically a telephone with a small attached computer screen and keyboard. This device is already being piloted in New York, with 324 customers, and is being launched more widely in 1992.

Citibank home banking executives say that home banking customers generate, on average, $100 more in profit per year than other customers. However, since Citibank is believed to have spent millions of dollars in developing the Enhanced Telephone, the bank is clearly still some way from making telephone banking profitable in its own right, if that were an objective.

Smart cards

Smart cards are not yet making any kind of impact on the US financial scene. A source at Bank Network News – a leading research organization for the US electronic payment systems scene – said that at present, the widespread deployment of smart card implementations in the US was apparently being prevented by a simple cost factor: that smart cards cost about twice as much as magnetic cards. However, there are nonetheless many commercial organizations in the US working on smart card applications across a variety of fields and my hunch is that sooner rather than later we will see some interesting pilot implementations of smart cards taking place in the US.

CONTINENTAL EUROPE

BELGIUM

Automated Teller Machines

The major operator of ATMs in Belgium is the Brussels-based Banksys, which runs a network of about 900 ATMs (expected to grow to 1000 by early 1992). These ATMs are owned by 69 Belgian banks.

There are also another 150 lobby ATMs which are not part of the Banksys systems and which are operated privately by the leading banks.

About 4.8 million ATM cards are issued to a population which is in the vicinity of 10 million.

There were formerly two ATM networks in Belgium, Banksys and Mr Cash. However, these merged in 1989, although the brandings 'Bancontacta' (the Banksys branding) and 'Mr Cash' remain on all ATM cards.

Electronic Funds Transfer at Point of Sale

EFTPoS is well advanced in Belgium, with around 29 000 outlets where cards can be used. The number of outlets is growing rapidly. All ATM cards are also EFTPoS cards. In addition to credit card schemes operated by international players Visa and Eurocard, Banksys operates the EFTPoS system.

Telephone banking

Telephone banking is spreading rapidly around Belgium, although there are (as yet) no branchless banks in the country. Five leading Belgian banks offer telephone banking services, including General de Banque and CGEK. This service involves a customer having access to account details via a touch tone telephone. The number of customers who have accounts to which a telephone banking facility is attached is currently around 3 million.

Smart cards

There are not yet any major smart card initiatives in the Belgian banking scene.

FRANCE

Automated Teller Machines

French ATMs are operated by Cartes Bancaires, which currently runs 14 800 ATMs, all of which are shared by the card-issuing banks. There are in the vicinity of 19.8 million Cartes Bancaires cards in circulation.

Electronic Funds Transfer at Point of Sale

EFTPoS is highly developed in France, a further indication of the gusto with which the French tend to apply useful new technology. There are currently about 500 000 EFTPoS terminals in France: almost ten-times the number that there are in the US for a country with a population a quarter of that in the US. Of these 500 000 terminals, 200 000 are completely electronic and account for about 80% of all transactions, with the other 300 000 using manual transaction slips.

Telephone banking

The French telephone banking scheme – Minitel – is based around the Minitel terminal, a dedicated PC system. A source at Cartes Bancaires said that the Minitel system was 'not yet' a major force in French banking, although he suggested that it was set to expand significantly in the future.

Smart cards

France is more advanced than any other European country – and probably more than any other country in the world – in terms of smart card implementation within the financial sector. Already 7 million Cartes Bancaires cards are smart carts, and in 1992 Cartes Bancaires will have completed the conversion of all its cards to smart cards. The Cartes Bancaires source said that the principal application of smart cards to date was to greatly increase the security of cards, as smart cards are in effect impossible to copy.

GERMANY

Automated Teller Machines

There are about 7300 ATMs in Germany. These can be used with Eurocheque cards and banks' own ATM cards. Of these ATMs 1500 can also be used with Eurocard.

All German ATMs are linked to each other, although the network does not have a particular branding. Forty million Eurocheque and ATM cards are issued for use in ATMs.

Electronic Funds Transfer at Point of Sale

The main German EFTPoS system is called 'Electronic Cash'. It has 7500 terminals, the majority of them located at petrol stations. These terminals can be operated by 25 million Eurocheque cards (with a Personal Identification Number) and 5 million credit cards (with signature verification).

Telephone banking

All German banks offer a home banking service that is branded as 'Btx-Homebanking'. This provides information about the state of an account and also allows account holders to initiate credit transfers from home. In order to participate in this service, the account holder needs a PC with a modem, Btx-software and a Btx-decoder.

Smart cards

To date, smart card initiatives in Germany have been experimental schemes only. For example, there has been a pilot scheme with smart cards at a shopping centre in Regensburg and a test combining smart card facilities with Btx-Homebanking technology in Paderborn. Readers seeking up-to-date information about smart card deployment in Germany should contact: ZKA, c/o Bundesverband der Deutschen Volksbanken und Raiffeisenbanken e.V, Heussallee 5, 5300 Bonn 1, Germany.

THE NETHERLANDS

Automated Teller Machines

There are currently about 11 million plastic cards issued in The Netherlands. These act as both ATM cards and EFTPoS cards. The Netherlands has an unusually large number of retail banks, about 50, for a population of 14 million. The ATM system – which operates about 2500 ATMs – is run by the leading ten banks, but accepts all banks' cards.

Electronic Funds Transfer at Point of Sale

EFTPoS is already quite highly developed in The Netherlands and is set on a rapid growth course. The national EFTPoS system is 'Beanet', which currently operates about 2600 terminals. This, according to a source at Beanet, will grow to around 3500 by the end of 1992, based on existing contractual arrangements. Beanet terminals accept all the plastic cards issued by Dutch banks.

Telephone banking

Telephone banking is still in the early growth phase in The Netherlands, although it is clear that this growth is likely to be rapid. There are currently two major telephone banking schemes: 'Girotel', which is a telephone-based system for private individuals and small businesses, and which has about 30 000 participants; and 'Electronic Banking', a PC-based system, run mainly for businesses, by seven leading Dutch banks, with a few thousand businesses participating at present.

Smart cards

The Netherlands has taken to smart cards with some enthusiasm. The major pilot scheme at present is a retail scheme being run by several Dutch banks and 200 retailers in the town of Woerden, near Utrecht. The pilot's 10 000 card holders make it currently one of the largest pilots in Europe.

There are two other pilot projects taking place. One is a scheme to investigate the extent to which smart cards can make an electronic payment system more secure. This is being operated by Girocentrale. The other pilot is an internal scheme being run by Bank Giro in its canteen to test the effectiveness of smart cards when used as an electronic purse.

PORTUGAL

Automated Teller Machines

The operator of the Portuguese ATM network (of 1150 ATMs) is Sociedade Interbancaria de Servicos S.A. (SIBS), which is owned by 26 Portuguese banks. The only ATMs in Portugal which are not run by SIBS are the banks' lobby ATMS, which are operated by the banks themselves.

At the end of August 1991 there were 3.2 million plastic cards issued by the Portuguese banks to run on the SIBS ATM network. This network bears the branding 'Cash Multibanco'.

Electronic Funds Transfer at Point of Sale

Portugal has a flourishing EFTPoS system. This is also operated by SIBS, and bears the branding 'TPA (i.e. POS) Multibanco'. There are currently about 8200 TPA Multibanco terminals in Portugal, for a population of ten million. The implementation of EFTPoS terminals is proceeding rapidly.

Telephone Banking

Telephone banking has yet to make a significant impact on the Portuguese electronic payments scene. There are currently two services, operated by the banks PPA and BCI, respectively. These services are still in the early growth phase and have yet to obtain a significant client base.

Smart cards

There are no pilot smart card schemes within the Portuguese electronic payments scene at present.

SPAIN

Automated Teller Machines

There are three ATM networks. These are:

TELEBANCO 4B with about 4000 ATMs. This network is managed by SISTEMA 4B;
RED 6000, with about 10 000 ATMs, managed by Savings Banks (CECA);
SERVIRCED with about 3000 ATMs, managed by SEMP.

These three networks are all interconnected and they accept every Spanish debit card, and some international cards via international ATM sharing.

Electronic Funds Transfer at Point of Sale

There are also three schemes, corresponding to the ATM schemes, as follows:

TELEPAGO 4B (run by SISTEMA 4B)
Savings Bank networks
SEMP network.

The total number of EFTPoS terminals in Spain is at present about 300 000. The vast majority of these are shared by the three EFTPoS networks.

Telephone banking

The principal telephone banking scheme in Spain at present is called DIRECTO and is operated by Banco Exterior de Espana.

Smart card

There are no significant smart card pilot schemes in Spain's retail financial sector at present.

CHAPTER EIGHT

Electronic payment systems from the customer's point of view

INTRODUCTION

In the film *Tin Men*, which stars Richard Dreyfuss and Danny De Vito as two salesmen of the early 1960s, the characters played by Dreyfuss and De Vito devote much of their energy to constructing elaborate scams designed to part gullible home-owners from their money. The two salesmen take it for granted that their product – aluminium sidings (strips which are bonded onto the outer walls of houses) – is fundamentally unattractive and can only be made appealing through chicanery. The film depicts the changing mood of the times by showing how the newly-formed US Home Improvements Commission impinges on the salesmen's lives, investigates their deceit and takes their licences away. The last few frames of the film show the Dreyfuss and De Vito characters, now both jobless, driving away from the Commission's investigation, and the Dreyfuss character noticing a Volkswagen in the street, and thinking about how this might represent a more reliable sales prospect than aluminium sidings. The Volkswagen is clearly used here as a symbol of a product that the public actually wants, and the upbeat note on which the film ends suggests that the future for the Dreyfuss and De Vito characters is going to consist of meeting the customers' real needs, not cheating them into buying something that they do not require.

We are all now familiar with the philosophy that business

can only succeed by meeting customers' requirements. It is easy to forget that this philosophy is a relatively recent one, and one that is a natural consequence of the growing affluence which has marked the industrialized nations since the 1960s. However, it might reasonably be argued that the financial sector, always more conservative than the rest of the business world, only began to put this philosophy into action during the 1980s, and that even now many retail financial institutions have yet fully to understand that they can only prosper by keeping their customers happy.

PRINCIPAL CONSUMER ADVANTAGES OF USING ELECTRONIC PAYMENT SYSTEMS

I would suggest that electronic payments systems can help institutions meet their customer's needs by the following principal methods:

1. by extending normal branch opening hours, thereby giving the customer greater flexibility;
2. by reaching into a wide variety of retail outlets (e.g. via EFTPoS) to provide customers with a convenient way to pay for things;
3. providing a level of impersonality which many customers appreciate (e.g. if checking a balance, many customers may prefer to be informed of a low or debit balance by an ATM or an automated telephone system rather than by a human teller);
4. because electronic payment systems are quicker and more accurate than human tellers;
5. access to electronic payment systems is often regarded by consumers as conferring status;
6. as in international ATM sharing, electronic payment systems offer great potential advantages to customers wishing to access their bank accounts overseas;
7. they allow younger, computer-literate customers to see financial institutions as dynamic, vibrant and exciting

organizations (whereas traditionally financial institutions were none of these things);

8. they provide financial institutions with opportunities to compete over the entire range of retail financial services provided, with inevitable benefits for customers.

ACCEPTING THE PRIMACY OF THE CUSTOMER

Making the most of electronic payment systems, however, is more than a matter of recognizing the benefits which these systems can give to an institution's customers.

What is needed from the institution is an entire customer-oriented business philosophy; a philosophy which should have its outworkings in every aspect of the institution's operations, from procedural and operational methods, staff training, and through to branch design and deployment of electronic payment systems.

Putting this philosophy into action sounds easy, but it isn't – see below.

FACTORS INHIBITING RE-ORIENTATION AROUND CUSTOMER NEEDS

Among the obstacles in the way of a customer-orientated business philosophy are the following.

1. Financial institutions consider that customers are often unreasonable.
2. Financial institutions consider that customers are sometimes dishonest.
3. Redesigning branches and implementing electronic payment systems is expensive.
4. Bankers tend to be conservative and are likely to resist in-depth changes to procedures and operations.
5. Many staff simply cannot be bothered.

Five obstacles – and five refutations – as follows.

1. **Financial institutions consider that customers are often unreasonable.** And so they are. But are you certain that what you consider 'unreasonable' doesn't really mean 'likely to make my job more difficult and cause me extra trouble?' After all, customers are not profit-generating objects, but people. Generally speaking, their desire for a personal level of service will always exceed what the financial institution is able, or willing, to provide. The solution? Try to meet customer needs more precisely, and design service infrastructures which can easily accommodate exceptional requests.

2. **Financial institutions consider that customers are sometimes dishonest.** And so they are. Of course you must make your systems secure. But you must find ways of doing that without alienating your customers – the vast majority of whom are not dishonest.

3. **Redesigning branches and implementing electronic payment systems is expensive.** Too bad. Do it, or perish.

4. **Bankers tend to be conservative and are likely to resist in-depth change to procedures and operations.** No one is suggesting that you abandon the procedures which years of experience have shown to be effective. But are you sure that the criterion for deciding whether a procedure is effective is that it allows you to give a better service, or that it simply makes your job easier? If it's the latter, it may be worth looking at.

5. **Many staff simply can't be bothered.** They'd better start to learn to be bothered, or find alternative employment.

IS THE CUSTOMER ALWAYS RIGHT?

So, is the customer always right? At an individual level, no. Customers make mistakes, act dishonestly, mismanage their finances, abuse staff. At an individual level, customers must sometimes be dealt with firmly but tactfully. After all, there isn't much point giving customers what they want if that puts you out of business.

But at a generic level, customers are always right because the only way for your institution to succeed in today's highly competitive climate is to provide a banking service that keeps existing customers contented and willing to come back for more, and which wins new customers. That is the only way. You can rationalize and cut costs until you and your colleagues are blue in the face, but that won't make your institution succeed if you're not giving your customers what they want in terms of banking services. Which is precisely why electronic payment systems are so important, because their deployment can greatly enhance the level of customer service which you provide. In these terms, electronic payment systems are like metal boxes of concentrated customer satisfaction.

TALKING TO JEREMY MITCHELL

Jeremy Mitchell might be described as one of the referees of the retail banking scene. A consumer watchdog of worldwide renown, Jeremy is an independent consumer policy adviser to international organizations, governments and consumer bodies. He is the author of *The European Dimension** and *A Consumer View of the Single European Market for Financial Services*†. He is also a member of the European Commission Payment Systems Users' Liaison Group.

His is a powerful, sincere voice which has influenced many governments, financial institutions, systems houses and consultants. I asked him for his views on what he considered areas of particular interest relating to how financial institutions are managing their relationships with consumers in terms of electronic payment systems. He chose initially to focus on the way in which debit cards are issued.

*Jeremy Mitchell (1989) *The European Dimension*, Policy Studies Institute, London.
†Jeremy Mitchell (1991) *Banker's Racket or Consumer Benefit? – A consumer view of the single European Market for financial services*, Policy Studies Institute, London.

This is what he had to say:

A few weeks ago I received some material from a financial
institution, inviting me to open a current account with
them. The leaflet explained that on opening the account I
would be given a card which would serve as an ATM
card, cheque guarantee card and Switch EFTPoS card. I
telephoned the institution to ask whether it was possible
to have an ATM card and cheque guarantee card without
the EFTPoS card. The institution's reply was that this was
not possible; if I wanted to open an account with them, I
had to have a card with an active direct debit function,
whether I wanted it or not. Nor was it possible for me to
get the direct debit function blocked off.

I then checked with my wife, who has a current account
with another institution. She discovered that her combined ATM card and cheque guarantee card also had a
Switch EFTPoS function. She had never asked for this. It
was issued as a replacement card by the bank in question.

These two incidents led me to a clearer understanding
of the extraordinary fact that there are now [June 1991]
more than 20 million debit cards issued in the UK, compared with 19 million at the end of 1990 and 13.5 million
at the end of 1989. It is small wonder that the UK Association for Payment Clearing Services (APACS) is able to
predict that 'it is probable that a large majority of current
account holders will hold a debit card within a few years'.
It seems pretty clear to me that the distribution of debit
cards – or rather, payment cards that include a debit function – has been the biggest inertia selling operation in
banking history.

It is probably now too late to ask whether this selling
operation should have been allowed to take place, or
whether – as happened in the 1970s after the initial unsol-
icited distribution of credit cards – it should have been
prohibited by statute. It is, however, *not* too late to ask
whether consumers should be denied the freedom to
choose whether they want a debit card function or not –

especially as the terms and conditions covering most debit cards impose obligations and liabilities on the consumer with which he or she may not wish to be burdened.

Now that the cards have been distributed in huge numbers, the question is whether consumers will use them. APACS figures show some 60 million debit card transactions in 1989 and 192 million in 1990. Some crude arithmetic suggests that the number of debit transactions per issued card averaged about 6 in 1989 and just under 12, or one a month, in 1990.

This represents a satisfactory increase in usage, certainly, but it is still at a very low level. Is the increase in usage of debit cards likely to grow fast enough to sustain an APACS forecast – revised downwards, incidentally – that 3 billion debit card transactions would take place each year by the end of this century? I am very much aware of how much importance the banks attach to persuading consumers to change from cheque payments to card payments. If they are not successful in persuading consumers to do this, then the payments side of banking will continue to be a drag on the profitability of retail banking, and banks are becoming increasingly dependent on profits from retail banking to compensate them for their appalling experience with Third World lending and some aspects of corporate banking.

So, banks and other financial institutions are currently giving a great deal of thought to a fundamental question: can consumers be persuaded that it is in their own interests to use debit cards?

If we look first at the balance of advantage between using a credit card and using a debit card, it seems most unlikely that there will be any massive shift away from credit cards towards debit cards. Unless someone is right up against his or her credit card limit, or is finding it difficult to repay outstanding credit card debts, the debit card offers no advantage. The credit card, by contrast, offers a grace period, even if that is currently under pressure, and far from working in favour of debit card usage, annual fees for credit cards actually strengthen the case for using a credit card, in terms of getting 'value for money' for your credit card fee by spreading its use over as many transactions as possible.

Turning to the balance of pros and cons of debit cards as against cheques, the market research results of which I am aware suggest that the main advantage of the debit card is convenience and simplicity – rather amorphous concepts, but none the less significant. Cashback is another distinct advantage.

However, against these, using a cheque brings some very positive advantages. In the UK, our cheque guarantee card system ensures that a card-backed cheque is an almost universally acceptable means of payment. Acceptability is not selective and does not depend on which bank or building society's name is at the top of the cheque. When using a debit card, however, the consumer has no advance assurance that the means of payment will be acceptable. He or she has to look for the logo.

A further disadvantage of using a debit card is that the consumer protection framework attached to its possession and use is inferior to the legal protection that the consumer has when paying by cheque. Banks and building societies have made a basic error in getting their lawyers to draw up terms and conditions for the use of payment cards in a way that is highly protective of the interest of the financial institutions concerned, and detrimental to the interests of consumers.

The one-sided character of payment card terms and conditions has been fully set out elsewhere, for example, in the Jack Report, and it is a major failure of the banks and building societies that they have not taken the message to heart in drafting the Code of Practice which is supposed to take account of the Jack Committee recommendations and the Government White Paper and give consumers a better deal, which in its present form patently does not.

So far as the float (i.e. the period, if any, between when a transaction is completed and when payment is debited from the customer's account) is concerned, there is currently no difference from the consumer viewpoint, in that the account debiting period for debit cards is aligned with that for cheques. However, this constitutes potential vulnerability for the consumer when using a debit card. In their never-ending search for ways of widening their margins, banks may at some time in the future change to instant debiting of debit card payments. All that float waiting to be captured must be a great temptation.

I would conclude by saying that, at present, paying by debit card seems to offer the consumer few, if any, advantages. For the consumer who pays by credit card, there is a definite disadvantage in changing to debit card payment, as the money leaves the consumer's account sooner. For the consumer who pays by cheque, the plus of simplicity is more than balanced by the minuses of loss of universality and a significantly lower level of consumer protection.

I believe that if the use of debit cards is to become a really major method of payment, then the minimum improvements that need to be made are:

◆ acceptance of debit cards at all terminals, irrespective of the logo on the card;
◆ improvements in card terms and conditions to meet the Jack Committee recommendations.

Over and above these minimum improvements, however, there needs to be a positive incentive for consumers to use debit cards. This should be a clear plus in terms of money or convenience, which is missing at the moment. This will be needed if consumers are to be persuaded to change from their existing payment methods.

It is salutary for those who are closely and professionally involved in innovations in payment methods to remember that the overwhelming majority of consumers are not in the slightest degree interested in making payments as such. Their approach is instrumental – you make a payment in order to get something.

In the words of the Banking Ombudsman:

> Customers do not use banks because they want to, but because they are a necessary evil. The customer who savours a good wine derives no pleasure from the plastic card used to buy it. His pride in his home will not extend to the mortgage with which it was acquired, let alone to the bank which made the advance. Primarily, what a bank has to offer is service, and it is on service, not product, that the emphasis should lie.
>
> The challenge for banks and building societies is to convince consumers that debit cards provide a service which has recognizable and tangible advantage compared with other methods of payment. At present, in common with the great majority of consumers, I remain a sceptic.

In a wider context, I also discussed with Jeremy Mitchell his more general views regarding the impact of plastic cards on consumers*. This is what he had to say:

> The plastic card revolution has brought benefits to many consumers. Using a cheque guarantee card gives the retailer the assurance of a bank guarantee of payment and reduces the uncertainty or embarrassment of a cheque being refused. It is now easier for us to get at our money by withdrawing cash from ATMs, especially during the evenings and at weekends, when banks are closed. The specific advantages of EFTPoS are less clear, but market research by banks shows that some consumers find it more convenient than paying by cash or cheque. There is now a much wider choice of payment methods open to consumers than there was 20 – or even ten – years ago.
>
> There are, however, some problems. While the great majority of card transactions go through without difficulty, a small minority cause considerable trouble. For example,

*Jeremy Mitchell (1991) *Banker's Racket or Consumer Benefit? – A consumer view of the single European Market for financial services*, Policy Studies Institute, London.

in the UK, complaints about disputed card transactions constitute the largest single category of complaints received by both the banking Ombudsman and the Building Societies' Ombudsman. Card problems have been a focus of attention for Denmark, France, Germany, The Netherlands and Spain. These problems have now been taken up on the EC level.

The principal problems encountered by consumers include the following:

- consumers may be sent payment cards and/or PINs even though they have not asked for them;
- consumers may not be given enough information about their rights and responsibilities when using cards;
- there may be a lack of clarity about the precise moment at which a payment card contract comes into force;
- consumers may not be given a printed record of a payment card transaction;
- payment card contracts are drawn up unilaterally by the card issuer;
- card issuers often make unilateral changes to the terms of the contract and often without giving consumers adequate notification of the changes;
- contracts may be written in obscure legal language;
- consumers are frequently held liable for the unauthorized use of payment cards when they have been lost or stolen, sometimes even after loss or theft has been notified by the card issuer; their accounts are debited with transactions carried out by others without their knowledge and authorization;
- some card issuers do not provide adequate round-the-clock facilities to enable consumers to report the loss or theft of cards;
- when a consumer disputes whether a transaction has taken place or whether it was authorized, he or she is often faced with an impossible burden of proof;

◆ card issuers often disclaim liability for consumer losses caused by faults in their systems or equipment;

◆ in many EC member countries, there are no cheap, rapid and effective procedures for resolving disputes between the consumer and the card issuing organization.

This long catalogue of consumer problems with cards would not matter so much if there was effective consumer protection legislation which dealt specifically with payment cards, but, with the sole exception of Denmark, this is not the case. In other EC countries some aspects of payment card usage are caught accidentally by legislation designed primarily for other purposes. Otherwise, consumers' use of payment cards is governed by the contracts drawn up by card issuers. Only in The Netherlands are these negotiated between the consumer organizations and the banks; elsewhere they are issued unilaterally and are invariably one-sided. The unfairness to the consumer of the great majority of these contracts is well known.

However, Jeremy also points out that the European Commission is currently spearheading an initiative to standardize payment system contracts throughout EC Member States, and in particular to lay down and implement specific recommendations for making the 'balance of power' in these contracts between consumer and institution more equitable. Details of the recommendations have yet to be finalized, but it is likely that by around 1993 institutions will be obliged to approach the business of drawing up these kind of contracts with much more caution and respect for the consumer. In the meantime, institutions which wish to demonstrate that they are 'consumer-friendly' rather than simply asserting that they are, may well find that they can establish a competitive advantage over their rivals in this respect by seeking to enter into fairer contracts with their consumers now, rather than waiting for legal statutes which compel them to do so.

CONCLUSION: THE NEED FOR A CUSTOMER RELATIONS STRATEGY

The conclusion to this chapter ought to be self-evident. If your institution is not already developing a coherent across-the-board strategy on customer relations – a strategy directed both at improving the level of customer service and also maintaining a policy of transparently fair dealing with consumers in such matters as the issuing of debit cards – then you might consider that, as your rival institutions are probably developing such strategies, you may be at a distinct disadvantage to them.

CHAPTER NINE

The future of electronic payment systems

INTRODUCTION

Making an informed forecast of the state of the electronic payments systems scenario in the future should at best consist of assessments of likely future trends rather than predictions of actual future events. Free-ranging speculation is likely to lead to mistaken conclusions and overlooked possibilities. Extrapolating existing trends into the future, however, may well furnish reliable predictions of future scenarios.

In any event, while it is reasonable to consider that the impact which electronic payment systems have made on people's lives in most of the developed world during the past twenty years – and especially the last ten years – have indeed been revolutionary, it is probably the case now that the process of change within the electronic payment systems industry has become that of a rapid evolution rather than a revolution.

The following is a summary of some of the most important major trends within the electronic payment systems arena at present. I list them in the order of the importance which I attach to them, although I should emphasize that this order of importance is only personal, and the reader may well disagree with me.

1. **Increased customer willingness to accept electronic payment systems**
   Above all, it is highly likely that customer willingness to

accept with enthusiasm those electronic payment systems
which offer convenience, useful functions and a high degree
of information will continue to increase. This is the simple
extrapolation of a trend which has been evident since the
mid-1970s: consumers like electronic payment systems and
find them quick and convenient. However, there is the
important proviso – and one that I have emphasized
throughout this book – that the genesis of the electronic
payment system must be that it fills a real gap in the market
in terms of convenience, speed and information, and ideally
all three. As this book has repeatedly emphasized, an electronic payment system which is introduced simply because
it is an innovation is not likely to make its mark on the
market, either now or in the future.

2. **A greater recognition among retail financial institutions of
the importance of accommodating consumer rights**
Retail financial institutions are slowly starting to recognize
that not only must they deploy electronic payment systems
which met real customer needs, but they must also do
more than pay lip-service to consumer rights. As far as
accommodating consumer rights is concerned, institutions
have all too often in the past adopted a 'mandarin'-like
approach that, as major financial institutions they can never
make mistakes and that the consumer must always be
wrong when disputes occur. In the past, the adoption on
the part of institutions of such a rigid attitude to consumer
matters has to some extent reduced consumer respect and
liking for electronic payment systems and in some cases
introduced a completely unnecessary level of tension in the
institution–consumer relationship. This is not, of course, to
say that institutions should not create procedural infrastructures which allow them to protect their assets and their
members' or shareholders' interests, but I do think that
those institutions which are seen to have an active interest
in creating good relations with consumers will ultimately
have an important edge over those institutions which do
not do this. In any event, the type of institution–consumer
problems which Jeremy Mitchell identified in Chapter Eight

are likely, during the next few years, to be made the subject of European Community-wide legislation which stipulates exactly how far an institution may go. Surely it is best for an institution to anticipate this legislation, and become known as a 'consumer-friendly' institution sooner rather than later?

3. **Greatly increased network sharing within and across national borders**

This is perhaps the most immediately obvious opportunity to extrapolate current trends into future scenarios. Institutions' desire to cut the costs of deploying electronic payment systems and at the same time increase the level and range of services which they offer their customers means that they have every reason to participate in sharing agreements both within their own country and also with institutions in other countries. Indeed, since national sharing is already highly developed, the greatest scope for expansion naturally lies within international sharing.

There are, unfortunately, still many obstacles to the creation of a scenario where national and international sharing can proceed with maximum speed. Perhaps one of the most substantial obstacles is that of the relative lack of technical and legal standards. However, here again the European Community is mounting a major initiative, through a number of advisory bodies, to create common standards throughout the Community for standardization and to break down other obstacles. Provided that the sharing will have definite benefits both for the participating institutions and their customers, I believe that with the advent of the new EC legislation international sharing will accelerate.

One result of this is likely eventually to be a 'shake-out' of financial institutions, as the infrastructure created by the sharing suggests new organizational structures for the participating institutions. As well as leading to new mergers and takeovers between institutions located in the same country, we are also likely to see scenarios where institutions from different countries may themselves merge – at least as far as national legislation permits this.

4. **Further developments in electronic technology**
   Electronic payment systems are obviously facilitated in a
   purely technical sense by developments in technology, and
   during the next few years I expect to see a great surge in
   the breadth of the services that are available to customers
   via ATMs, EFTPoS and telephone banking systems. I also
   expect to see smart cards reach maturity as a technology,
   thus opening up the concept of the 'portable bank', whereby
   a customer can almost literally carry his or her bank around
   with him or her, with the 'bank' being able to do everything
   in terms of providing up-to-date account information. This
   information could be updated by the smart card being
   inserted into a branch-based terminal or a terminal which
   could be located inside the customer's home (or even inside
   his or her briefcase), and which could be updated remotely.
   The smart card/portable banking facility could, indeed, do
   everything besides dispense cash, and even this may cease
   to be a problem if the smart card could be 'loaded' remotely
   with credits, which would then be consumed when the
   smart card was used to activate the provision of a particular
   service or product.

5. **The rise of the financial markets in eastern Europe**
   Political changes in eastern Europe during the late 1980s
   and early 1990s have meant that the days when eastern
   Europe was regarded as a marginal region with little interest
   in developing sophisticated retail financial services infrastructures are already over. The years to the mid-1990s are
   likely to see an unprecedented level of activity within eastern Europe banking markets, as these countries prepare
   themselves for what must be their ultimate goal: membership of the European Community. During this period I
   think the appetite of eastern European banks' customers
   for electronic payments systems will become increasingly
   voracious, and while, certainly a great deal of work must
   be undertaken by these new-style market economy banks
   in order for them to create the infrastructures which will in
   due course carry electronic payment messages, the creation

of these infrastructures will surely happen sooner rather than later.

CONCLUSION

Bearing the above five major trends in mind, there is every reason to expect that ATMs, EFTPoS, telephone banking and smart cards will become even more important within the retail financial sector than they already are. Not only this, but the electronic payment systems arena will become even more interesting and challenging than it has proved itself to be in the past, as financial institutions throughout the world strive to plan and implement electronic payment systems which meet the requirements of existing customers and attract new customers, thereby boosting customer satisfaction and institutions' profits.

Glossary

ATM sharing   The sharing of ATMs (q.v.) or an ATM network (q.v.) with other institutions. The rationale for ATM sharing is that the high capital costs of installing an ATM, and the environmental and practical objections to the proliferation of large numbers of ATMs within proprietary networks, gives financial institutions every reason to share their ATMs with each other, particularly since modern switching (q.v.) technology allows transactions to be kept fully secure and confidential. All shared ATM networks report continually increasing volumes of transactions across the network by customers of one institution using an ATM owned by another institution.

Automated Teller Machine (ATM)   Popularly known as a 'cash machine', an ATM is an automatic device for dispensing cash and a variety of other banking services to a bank's customers. It is usually activated by a customer's plastic card (q.v.) used in conjunction with a PIN (q.v.). There are two main types of ATMs: lobby machines, which are usually located in the lobby of a financial institution, although sometimes lobby ATMs are placed inside retail establishments, such as supermarkets; and 'through-the-wall' ATMs, which are located in the walls of institution's branches, and can thus be used by customers even when the branch is closed.

Electronic Funds Transfer at Point of Sale (EFTPoS)   A system for allowing a customer to pay for goods by arranging for his or her account to be debited once the transaction has been made. Some EFTPoS systems debit instantaneously, whereas others provide a 'float', consisting of a time-lag which may be an overnight delay, although it is more likely to be three days (the normal clearing period for a cheque). EFTPoS systems are typically operated by the customer presenting a plastic card at the point of sale, with PIN(q.v.)-based verification or signature verification.

Electronic payment system   Any electronic system, which will typically consist of a central computer connected remotely to a number of dedicated computer terminals, which allows a financial institution's customer to communicate with the institution and make payments and other transactions.

Network   Any kind of electronic communications system between computers which allows an electronic payment system (q.v.) to function.

Personal Identification Number (PIN)   A number, usually four digits in length, which represents the security code of a plastic card (q.v.) and which must be used in conjunction with the card.

Plastic card   Any card which can be used in conjunction with an ATM (q.v.) or EFTPoS (q.v.) system. Plastic cards usually have a magnetic strip implanted on the back, which contains card-holder information. The plastic card is often referred to as an 'ATM card' when used in ATMs, and as a 'debit card' when used in an EFTPoS system.

Smart card   A smart card represents the next stage of technological development of the plastic card (q.v.). Instead of having a magnetic strip embedded in them, smart cards contain a microchip – essentially a miniature computer – which allows far more material to be stored on them, including a 'loading' of credit which can then be spent by the card holder. An extension of the smart card is the 'super-smart card', which is essentially a smart card with a set of alphanumeric and functions keys built in, allowing date to be inputted to the card by the card holder.

Switching   The process of routing electronic messages around a shared network in order that details of relevant transactions are routed to the host computer operated by the appropriate institution.

Telephone banking   A banking facility which can be accessed remotely by a customer via his or her telephone. Telephone banking usually provides the customer with access to a synthesized or digital voice via a touch tone pad. Voice response technology is also being used, but this is (as yet) insufficiently advanced to be very reliable. Although originally designed primarily to provide the customer with an up-to-date balance, telephone banking facilities are being widened to cover such additional functions as statement and cheque book ordering; the making of payments to third parties; and the opportunity to talk to an assistant if required.

Index